The road is long for a weary traveler

Find a shady spot to rest.

Put down the burden

that took a lifetime to gather

and dream once more.

September 2013

Home Again

Kate sat, wrapped in a blue plaid bathrobe, drawing deeply on her second cigarette in the past fifteen minutes. She sat silently in a suspended walkway between two wings of West Medical Center, as if trapped in a birdcage. As she gazed up toward the lights that shone down from the top of the Center, a fine dusting of powder drifted down in the deserted space below. One end of the walkway led to her ward while the other was attached to a solid brick wall where a large, gray, metal door was locked and chained with hardware so massive even the most psychotic patients barely glanced at its promise of escape.

She finished her cigarette, field stripped the butt, and watched the pieces swirl like seeds; scattering to the frozen grass two stories below. From her perch she swayed slowly side to side, watching the snow falling to the ground. Kate hoped to hear the little one out here. The noise and bustle inside the ward must have been frightening. So too would all the people. Inside she had tried to listen for her giggles that usually turned into peals of laughter, but with all the noise she couldn't focus long enough to pick them out of the air. She was ever hopeful that the child wasn't frightened by the flashing lights of the police cars and the long, sheering wail of the ambulances. She knew deep down she would see the fragile grey-eyed child again. If only she could be alone; the child would walk and laugh again.

Kate turned her ear to the wind, picking apart the sounds of the ward from the campus below. She let herself loose into long lost memories of endless treks, searching for what narrowly escaped her grasp. She saw herself waiting alone on a deserted beach, then following the child with cotton white hair through dimly lit trails under a casted moonlight. The more patient she was the longer the little one would stay with her. But Kate always had to be alone.

I showed her so much along the trails, she mused to herself. We were having fun until someone decided it was wrong. I should have known she would leave. She always does. Kate had stopped talking about the little one for some time, becoming accustomed to her daughters throwing long glances at each other when she did.

When she visited her parents, her sister called a play by play of her movements. That more than annoyed her. How could it not? She often thought,

"I wonder if I scratch my ass would my sister announce, "Hey, Kate's scratching her ass"?

"Honestly, who wouldn't light out of there in a hurry?" she asked herself. Crazy has nothing to do with it. And it was good to leave.

Kate kept her head cocked to the side, listening while mulling over what she had learned in the past four years. Even though she was new to this facility, her rules remained the same. She knew too much to get involved with the other patients. She bore scars from previous attempts to talk to or console others, and learned to stake a claim and ward off others from her room or possessions. Most of all, she learned to speak loudly and not back down. A habitual accounting of her cigarettes told her that she had enough to last until her sister, Karla, came to visit tomorrow afternoon. She could then continue to keep up her silent vigils.

The door to the ward opened to admit a young, good looking man-boy that Kate spent most of her two day stay in the halls of West avoiding. She was unnerved that he would bother her here. Now she knew that there was no sense in waiting for something that would no longer come. Faith would never appear to anyone but her and her alone.

The man-boy, Mikey, was a lost puppy. She ignored him at first but some maternal instinct, aided by the awareness of their predicaments, had allowed him some of her time. She tried to keep him occupied and at arm's length. She taught him a simple yoga routine which he turned into a competition. The young man, barely twenty, thought he could take her on. Once she demonstrated the routine he smiled and attempted the first pose. She could barely stifle a giggle while the athletic youth wiggled and shook. For amusement, Kate encouraged her charge to fall from one posture into the next. She had been patient at first but then, with a reassuring voice, she left him to his own devices.

For Kate, it was either becoming the boy's surrogate mother or giving him something to occupy himself then fade away. Although she had chosen the latter, he constantly sought her out.

Mikey greeted Kate with a big puppy grin. She weighed her options: with Mikey in the cage there would be a body to keep the smoking area open, but if she stayed it would mean a closer relationship than she was willing to allow. She stood up, and in one fell swoop greeted and dismissed him.

Kate grabbed the frozen handle of the door and swung it open. She felt the stifling heat of the Day Room rush her face and hands. The room was quiet and an ancient television screen reflected the heavy chairs and anchored table. A staff member sat behind a thick glass partition. He nodded slowly. She knew this movement meant he was making his presence known; he was watching her. Kate sauntered quietly past him, letting him know she was aware of *his* presence; but most of all, that she didn't care he was there or anywhere for that matter.

Once in her room Kate sat squarely on her single bed. A small black travel bag was open nearby. She eyed the case. "At forty-two," she thought, "this is sum of my life." She counted two worn pairs of Levis, a couple of summer shirts, and four giant bottles of shampoo with their corresponding giant bottles of conditioner, which were family donations, ranging from two dollar bottles to twenty dollar bottles. "Well," she thought to herself, "I can't say family doesn't care."

Earlier in the evening, Karla and her husband, Tom, came to see Kate. She waited patiently for the couple to pass security and watched them through the glass partition. She knew by Karla's posture that her sister had more in store than a brief family visit. Tom hugged Kate quickly and then sat in one of the bolted down chairs. Karla did not hug, touch or greet Kate, but firmly set to her mission. Her sister stood over her and her voice took a fevered pitch as she dug into Kate forcefully. Apparently Karla believed all Kate needed to be set back on course was a good talking to.

Kate let her grab a hold for about two sentences and then she let loose, telling herself: "What's the point of being mental if you can't let go every once in a while?" If Kate remembered correctly, her sister's face turned about three shades of red before she grabbed her designer purse from the visiting room table and stormed out. Tom remained behind. He hugged her and asked if there was any more she needed. She requested money for food: pizza to be exact. While he retrieved his wallet from his back pocket, she had taken the opportunity to let him know that the kitchen never delivered enough for the patients and the staff always made excuses. Tom didn't respond to Kate's announcement; instead, he hugged her tightly and slipped away.

Later that night Kate shared her pizza with patients in the ward who had been generous to her or in need themselves. She laughed to herself that sharing outside food required a serious covert operation. The pizza was delivered to the floor, and only after it passed security did it go to the admission nurse's station where she signed and paid for it. She then had to sneak it down the long hallway without drawing attention, then slip into her room and whisper to her group to come one by one. Tonight she had hidden a slice in the top drawer of her room's laminated dresser so she could savor the delicacy at her own leisure. There was always the possibility that a guest would take more than was fair and she might have to go without. She never opened herself up for this mistake on the inside, but in the outside world she often came up short.

Finally alone, Kate's stomach growled as the aroma of cheese and salty meats wafted from the drawer. She pulled the simulated wood grain drawer open revealing the still warm slice resting on a rusty, grease stained napkin. Ever mindful of the paths that had led her to these places in her life, tonight in her quiet room, Kate unleashed the heavy burden by savoring the treasure. She refused to let the reels replay in her head. Just for this one meal, she could put it all aside.

She was alone in room 524, quietly immersed in the taste and texture of the only thing that could bring her comfort and solace. She finished her slice and relished the feeling of falling asleep with the ease that only a full stomach could provide. She cinched the belt on her robe and crawled under the worn, light green blanket of the hospital bed. Lying on her side she gazed down on her worldly possessions and noticed a large brown teddy bear. His big red bow clashed in the muted solace of the clinical calm of the hospital room. She tried to remember where the bear came from…was it a gift…had she bought it during her travels…or was it even possible that her little one had left it behind? Kate searched inwardly, but could not focus on the memory. She fell asleep sifting.

Kate woke as soon as the first sunbeam faintly lit the room. She hurried to the day room with hopes of finding the food trays lined up on the counter. She walked in and glanced around. The faint scent of something eggy hung in the air, but she found the breakfast trays empty and neatly stacked at the end of the long counter. One lonely diner inhabited the room and in front of her young yoga prodigy sat were two trays. She sat down beside him. He ignored her presence and fitfully shoveled scrambled eggs into his mouth. She glanced at the slip on the tray closest to her and quickly recognized her name and patient number. Instead of being angry at the misappropriated food she said started slowly, "Men sure do eat a lot huh, Mikey?"

Mikey looked sideways at her. He realized the implication that he owed the older woman more than just exercise routines. He grabbed a plastic saucer of soggy toast and a plastic tub of jam and slid it off the tray toward her. She slowly reached up and quietly peeled back the silver top of the jam, spreading it thickly onto the soggy toast. While he started in on the soy sausage, she sat serenely next to him and savored the sugary fruit flavored bread as if it were her last meal.

Kate placed the last little morsel of sticky bread in her mouth. She grabbed a stray paper napkin from the chipped laminated table and held it to her lips. She cautiously held her body stock still as she watched a teddy bear bedecked, scrub covered woman approach her from the hallway. The woman had a serene look about her that read menacing to Kate's mind. Mikey finished their breakfasts, let out a resounding belch and headed for the walkway leaving the trays for Kate to dispose of properly under the plentiful gaze of the large day staff. He reminded her quietly that she owed him a showdown in the large front hall before he disappeared.

She was irritated with this announcement.

"That little shit," she thought.

"He eats my breakfast, gives me soggy bread and sugar, and I owe him. Asshole. Yep, men are assholes. They steal from you and then you owe them. They must learn it young, cuz they sure don't forget it when they are old."

Kate was ready to let out a rant but, considering she had not seen the quiet room at this facility, she swallowed her anger.

"Yeah," she thought "if you want to hear from me then you can't choose what I say."

Kate opened her mouth to speak the thought but suddenly felt a cool, almost cold, hand wrap around her wrist. The time had passed for her to shout to a room of note takers and patient reporters.

"Kate," she heard a too calm voice attached to the hand. Kate stilled her body to the cold vice that gripped her while beneath her seemingly calm exterior warning signals buzzed and clanged.

"You have been on the ward under observation for seven days. The board met early this morning to review your case."

Kate followed the hand on her wrist up the arm to the voice that seemed to suddenly have an opinion. She studied the face of the older woman now seated across from her. Who the hell is this woman? She thought. Kate had not seen her in the halls or the tiny glass closet, but she let her speak because this woman somehow thought it was important.

The woman continued, "I didn't agree with the decision that was made for your care. I thought you would be better served in a nearby facility. However, they are private institutions. We don't have any form of insurance for you. You have nothing in your personal effects and the people who admitted you said that you were admitted with only an ID and a few clothes. We've asked your family for the information and they have no knowledge of your health care arrangements. Unfortunately, we are going to have to send you to a state run facility."

Kate's head snapped back as though she had been slapped. She had insurance. She had good insurance. She took a minute to breathe.

"I'm sorry Ma'am, but I have insurance from my job. Didn't my girls tell you that? If I don't have my insurance card, can't you look it up?"

The woman who seemed to have nothing but patience took Kate's small wrist into her larger, if not stronger, hands and repeated the phrase just as delicately as she had before:

"I don't agree with the decision that was made for your care, but you don't appear to have any insurance, my dear."

The woman loosened her grip in an attempt to pat Kate's hand reassuringly as Kate swiftly disentangled herself from the gesture. Screech! Kate slid the chair loudly across the Day Room floor leaving the table and the harbinger behind.

Kate jammed her hands into the trusty pockets of her robe and rushed full force to the cage. Kate watched the deceivingly dressed figure stand and straighten her rumpled garment. Without a glance at Kate or the staff, the woman abruptly left the room. Just as Kate was unsure that she had ever seen the woman who appeared at her breakfast table, she was sure that she would never see her again

Kate spent most of her day being where other patients were not. In the late afternoon, she reluctantly fulfilled a promise. Kate met the six-foot-two swindler of meals in the large hall. Mikey was lean, cute, and only nineteen. During their continuing yoga practices on the worn grey carpet in the past week, Kate had lent an ear. He claimed he had a tricked out Jeep that his buddies were taking care for him, a pregnant 17 year-old girl friend, and a thriving meth trade. He also had a small addiction, still lived with his Mom who depended on him for financial support, and had a pending court date.

What Mikey talked about most was not letting his girlfriend take his car. Kate nodded dutifully and said "What's best for you?" She knew that the healing routine would not just pass time but would also calm and focus his though while lessening her own agitation. He only wanted to see was only interested in seeing which of the two could get through the routine with as little the least effort and as quickly as possible. In this Kate would not let him win. He could beat her to dinner breakfast, but she maintained her superiority in a routine that she had done every morning and every night for the past 6 years.

Sure, he thought a young man of his athletic background could beat a tiny woman of indiscernible age, but she knew he couldn't and that is what brought them together at least 3 times a day during their stay. He pitted his muscular youth against something he knew nothing about. He only wanted to win. In the end Kate always won out.

"Kate?" He began as they sat together alone amidst the residents milling about the floor, "I have court in the morning, do you think I'm ok?"

Kate took his bony strong, bony hands in her own small ones. She allowed herself to touch him just this once. "Well, Mikey, I'll tell you. You are definitely calmer now than when I first saw you. You can sit in one place and you can look me in the eye. You're a little shaky, see your hands? But I'd say you're better. I can't believe you do that shit anyway. Have you ever seen someone who has been doing it for a long time?"

He stared briefly at the floor then met her eyes. "Maybe," was all he let out. Suddenly, Kate's face became soft as she gazed at a young man who was not a man at all yet. Kate could not look past the slumped shoulders and the down turned face.

"Mikey, listen. I have been hospitalized with heavy meth users. You know how you can tell? Meth heads are bone skinny. They have no teeth if any. And they are constantly twitching and talking to themselves. Let me tell you something, okay? You can recover or live with a lot of things, but when you go down that path the only thing that makes you better is death. You've got a baby and a good life ahead of you. Tomorrow, go into the courtroom and promise the judge you'll go to NA once a day and twice on Sunday. Be with your girlfriend and drop your buddies off at your Mom's so they can take care of her. Be a good Father, a good husband if you want. Do what you can do. Be good at it. Get out of here and don't look back."

He studied her face for a minute. He saw something he had not seen in her: concern. Mikey was touched. He almost felt bad he put her on a vending machine diet. He looked deeper in to Kate's grey eyes and saw weariness, a deep sadness.

He reached out, "Kate I'm probably out of here tomorrow. That's what my lawyer says anyhow. What about you? Do you want me to talk to him for you?"

The softness left Kate's face. "Oh, I'm out of here tomorrow too."

The two sat still at the end of the large hall. The milling patients moved into the dining hall. Mikey for once overlooked the possibility of stockpiling trays for his evening meal. His mind shifted to his court hearing and how his attorney could work a deal. "Kate let's go smoke ok? I think we missed dinner."

Kate and Mikey spent their last night on the ward together. The snow melted. The evening felt slightly balmy with the two bundled up in flannel robes and heavy slippers. She noticed that he was showing a little layer of brownish-blonde fuzz bristling on his lower jaw. She became aware of the coarse hair on her legs rubbing on her jeans. The mismatched pair sat in silence drawing thoughtfully in a gray cloud of their own while others from the floor filed in and out, only to smoke and then return to the security of the day room. She relished the outdoors. The night was clear and the dark sky reflected the lights of the city. Mikey watched Kate's upturned face in the silence of the cage. He finally found the opportunity to ask the question that he felt compelled to ask the first time she stood over him and corrected his technique. "Kate, why are you here?"

Kate studied the red tip of her burning cigarette. She lifted the filtered end to her lips drawing deeply, tilting her head upward as she slowly released the gray smoke. Only then did she answer Mikey in a low measured voice, "I lost Faith, that's why."

Moving On

One of the male staff, the biggest, burliest one on the floor, woke Kate not quite two hours after she shuffled into her room and collapsed on the green blanketed bed. A combination of little food and many cigarettes had taken their toll. She had recently become used to sleeping sixteen out of twenty four hours of the day, but still slept lightly in her constrictive surroundings. She heard the brusque male voice softly requesting her to wake up turn into a demand with a little bit of a threatening overtone. She knew which staff could be ignored, smiled at, or jumped to and this was a jumping one. She forcefully willed herself out of the hospital bed. The gray winter sun had not graced her box yet.

She had silently nicknamed this staff member Big Boy and knew he did not play. He gruffly commanded her to get her belongings and meet him in the day room. She quickly complied. She waited quietly in the dimly lit day room, fighting to keep her eyes open. The backlights were on, and the glass closet held a sluggish staff member. She didn't hear a single cough, sniffle, or rustle on the ward, but at the end of the hall, she heard a rattle that became clearer and sharper.

She recognized the sound. She heard chains sing as corresponding footsteps made their way closer. Big Boy had company with him as he entered the day room. The man that walked in the room with Big Boy was, to her surprise, even bigger than the floor enforcer.

She gauged the man. He was big he and wore some kind of uniform, but in his hand was something that confused her. It was a black bag. It was similar to an old fashioned doctor's bag, but she knew instinctively that this man was not a physician of any manner. She sat silently cinching her costume tightly, resigned to the unknown.

Before long the stranger retrieved a set of nickel plated handcuff from the gaping black jaws. They were nothing new. She could throw off police issue cuffs in two minutes. Not that she would, but you always need an out she thought. The familiarity of the cold metal brought comfort instead of fear. She wondered if handcuffing a patient was even legal.

"Big Boy must have read my mind," she mused, "cuz that's the first time I've seen him smile all week."

Big Boy led his companion to her seat. She took a closer look at the man before her. He was wearing some sort of a black and white rent-a-cop uniform with a patch hand-sewn to the white short-sleeve shirt. The large bag and cuffs jingled when Rent-a-Cop dropped them unceremoniously in the empty chair beside her. She could see Big Boy put on his serious face just so no one could read how much he enjoyed this part of his job. Big Boy stood in front of her chair and cleared his throat auspiciously.

He began gruffly, "Kate this is Robert. He is transporting you to Brown State Hospital. In order to do this, he has to ensure that you will not harm yourself or others. Because you are a known flight risk, we have to take precautions that will insure that you do not take flight during transportation."

Kate was betting on the handcuffs but the lilt in Big Boy voice at the end his speech gave her reason to wonder. The question in her mind was immediately cleared up by the rabbit Rent-A-Cop pulled out his bag. She had never seen them in person, but recalled the device from prison movies. In her mind the heavy binding chains were saved for murderers and dangerous criminals. She was neither.

The shackles hanging from Rent-A-Cop's hand jingled and shone in the dim light of the day room. She could not hide. She could not run. She hastily considered the smoking cage nearby but it was padlocked at the other end. What could she do? This was decreed as in her best interest by a board of mental health care professionals. By all accounts society trusted these concerned caring people. Kate's experiences told her differently.

There are times when crying is okay. There are other times when screaming is required. She did neither. All she could do was submit to decisions made in her best interest as she had done many times before.

Rent-A-Cop quickly set to work. He put the left bracelet on first and, with a number of rapid clicks, he adjusted the cuff to her wrist, while wrinkling up his face and shaking his head. Without hesitation, he adjusted the cuff on her right wrist until he could hear no more sounds. He immediately grabbed the long gray chain, fitting one cuff to her denim clad ankle then threading the loose end over the cuffs, and securing the loose end to her unbound ankle.

Big Boy leaned back on the dining table and casually took in the sight. Kate refused to look him in the eye. She was afraid that he would find some satisfaction with whatever look she gave him. No doubt he would recall this scene at leisure, but that was even more than she wanted to think about. So, there she was; all one hundred and ten pounds of her, bound in fifty pounds of hardware while two huge men towered over her, watching closely for some break, some gleaning of her predicament. She gave them none. She gave them even less as she jangled down the hall of the 4th floor of West Medical Center. Walking was difficult, but she found out quickly how to carry the weight of the shackles in her hands while shuffling her feet.

The men walked along side, minding not to touch her. She shuffled as she hefted the weight of the chains, all the while holding her head high with her eyes focused on the elevator door. Rent-A-Cop took Big Boy's signed papers and swiped his badge on the door to exit. The elevator to the outside world stood open. Kate did her best to make a soundless, quick transition while her guard walked slowly at her side. Once inside the elevator, she no longer fought the hardware but managed time to look up. Waiting with them on the ride was a clean-cut fortyish gentleman wearing a tailored gray suit. Standing next to him was a well-dressed younger man, who was staring at the elevator floor. She watched the young man. She searched his down turned face. The doors closed on the silence.

"Ding!" the elevator chimed on the arrival of ground floor, and in surprise, the young man looked up. Kate was waiting and in a brief jerk of her head, she gave Mikey a final goodbye glance.

The ground was bare when Kate stepped into the outside world for the first time in over a week. Rent-A-Cop pointed at an old once faded blue minivan parked in the hospital loading zone. The "transport vehicle" looked like an old family car that had outlived its usefulness. She shuffled to the side door and waited patiently for her companion, who thought his first duty was to retrieve the parking placard from the front of the car, leaving her to stand before various hospital staff arriving or departing early morning shifts. Few of them looked her way. Those who did glance over the figure quickly noted the heavy bonds that bound the slight woman and quickly looked away. She waited for her captor in quiet shame. She had never endured such public humiliation before and wondered if the treatment equaled some crime she couldn't remember committing.

Kate's fingers tingled from the weight of the metal and the cold air that blew through the parking lot. Rent-A-Cop was taking his time unlocking the door. As Kate began to feel moisture dripping from her nose to her upper lip, the uniform finally swung the side door open. Rent-A-Cop stood facing her. It became apparent to Kate that he would not help with the burden he placed on her. Solemnly, she sat on the floor of the van and grabbed the chains, and swinging her legs to lie in front of her. Getting to her perch in the back of the coach required a number of crouching and shuffling maneuvers, but to her own satisfaction, they were also carried out in silence. The side door slammed shut.

Kate evaluated the interior of the vehicle. She saw a few well-loved dolls strewn around in the back and a meter mounted between the worn front seats. Kate thought, man there are better ways to get a cab. Then she smelled it: biscuits! Sitting in front of the meter between the two front seats was a white bag stamped with golden arches. Kate was suddenly happy. Maybe this ride isn't so bad after all, she reasoned, I get breakfast on the way. She giggled inwardly.

Rent-A-Cop got behind the seat and started the engine. He pulled out of the parking lot and slowly made his way out of the city. Kate nodded off. Her lack of sleep from the night before, mixed with the hum and vibration of the van, overcame her determination her to remain alert.

Kate found herself in her own brightly lit kitchen. It was late Sunday morning as was her routine. She was baking biscuits. She could tell from the golden aroma filling kitchen that it was almost time to take them out of the oven. The eggs were fluffy and the gravy ready. Her girls were sitting on the couch in the adjoining family room. The conversation between the three in the sun kissed room was light and loving as was often the case during these times. All were patiently waiting. Kate felt a tall dark figure enter the space. It hovered about her in the kitchen, poking into the pans on the stove and prodding her to do more, do better, do faster. He was silent, but he wasn't always there.

Kate woke to the rustle of a bag. Rent-A-Cop had emptied it silently while she slept. Kate almost wept out loud when she saw the crumpled McDonald's bag on the floor. Still she could feel her eyes were damp. To break the hunger pangs she sat up and looked out of the window. Nothing but vast furrowed fields studded with the occasional grain silo passed the fogged up window. Kate felt her bladder tightening, but she knew if the man did not have the compassion to share a biscuit, he would have no better stance on stopping for her to pee. Kate closed her eyes and laid her head again on the grimy velour seat. The winter wind picked up and began to push her transport back and forth on the narrow two lane highway. The back of the van got colder. Kate gave in once again. She slept.

The van stopped at the entrance of what appeared from Kate's confined seat to be some sort of compound. A little village arose from what appeared to be a desolate wasteland in the northern part of her home state. Barren fields flanked all sides of the little complex while a mass of brick buildings from bygone eras resembled various brick buildings huddled together. The many structures were connected by black paved roads dotted with naked trees, waving their branches in the cold north wind. As Kate craned her neck to see out of the fog smeared window of her carriage, she felt no warmth inside and saw no warmth outside. A tiny red brick building stood as sentry before the sprawling compound, lying in the vast landscape before her.

Kate was tired of the unknown. Every turn lay ahead dark and uncharted. Kate was to road worn to muster up courage or even anger. Every day for too many years she had wished for this little jaunt back to mental health to be over. And some days she swore she had reached that goal. This she told herself was not one of those days.

Her departure from the chained safety of her new captivity loomed closer. Her driver mumbled into a radio. Kate held her breath to hear, but knew the words weren't meant for her. The brakes squealed briefly and the van stopped. Rent-A-Cop pulled a clipboard from the adjacent seat, checked the meter that was no longer clicking and scribbled purposefully in a battered binder. At least, Kate thought, he wrote something. That was until he again muttered something again unintelligible from her vantage point.

She would have laughed at the sight of the burl, pink man rummaging through the nooks and crannies of the front of his very sad limo if she didn't have to pee so badly. As it was, she felt a little easier when the driver found the nub of a pencil that fell under his seat and was then able to clock his time. She still had to walk more than she felt comfortable just for the possibility of relief. Rent-A-Cop, or Bear as she had secretly renamed him, finally rolled himself out of the driver's seat. He quickly reappeared at the side door, and loudly banged it open.

The back of the cab was cold already, but the air that swept through the van drove the temperature down to freezing. Kate's eyes stung from the chill. She could tell from Bear's demeanor that he would not be so patient on this walk. Kate stepped into the late morning air. The pressure she had felt for the past hour had been replaced by an urgent need for warmth or at least cold that was not so bitter. Kate picked up her chains and hobbled even more quickly than she thought possible to the green door with a sign that proclaimed "Authorized Personnel Only."

Bear stamped his large booted feet on the concrete step. With one black leather gloved hand he pushed a bright red button on the green door with the other he patted his shoulder through his thick wool coat. Kate stood huddled in his shadow. The cuffs had chaffed her wrists, but the cold rendered her unprotected hands numb. She was unable to feel the frozen shackles which she clutched almost unknowingly before her. The warm blue wool blue plaid robe which had seen her through many a night on watch in the cage seemed to fail in light of its past glories. The slippers that covered her feet were shamed as the icy concrete of the step crept into her toes and forcefully made its way further up. Kate could do nothing but wait.

The green door swung open, and Bear rushed in. Kate entered slowly behind him, hobbled by the chains and beaten by the weather. A plump woman with dyed yellow hair, and glasses hung by a bedazzled chain, sat her thick self behind a desk. She motioned for the frozen woman to sit in the chair before her. Kate took her time crossing the room, but when she got to the chair Bear was on her. She watched as he retrieved the jewelry he had so cautiously bound her with earlier that morning. When she was free of the adornment, she did not rub her bruised wrist or stretch her cramped muscles. She simply looked at Bear. He would not meet her gaze. He busied himself packing away his devices and then stood silently looking away until he was able to catch Kate's new guardian in between shuffling stacks of papers.

Bear interrupted the clerk almost timidly.

"Uh Ma'am, I got some paperwork for you to sign real quick here."

He pulled out a well-worn log from his work gear.

"Ma'am if you could just initial the mileage on this paper and then sign at the bottom under authorization, I sure would appreciate it." He continued while pointing at a rumpled white sheet.

The yellow bee-hive woman looked up from her case file. She cocked her head in his direction.

Bear continued apologetically, "You know I gotta get paid Ma'am. You just sign this paper and I'll be on my way. Then you can take care of business, 'kay?"

From Kate's position she saw the woman squint her eyes at the bothersome man as though she was mulling over her options. She turned toward Kate and seemed to decide that she was going nowhere soon. The woman lifted her glasses off of her chest and grabbed the paper Bear had offered so politely. With a flourish of her almighty pen, she signed in the appropriate spaces, shoved the paper back in his waiting hands, minus one copy. Bear effortlessly filed the paper, grabbed his jingling bag and disappeared through the green door. All that marked his absence was a swirl of cold air.

The fussy, plump lady settled herself once again in her paperwork. Kate watched as she went through the file. Evidently, the woman didn't know she was waiting there. Kate waited. The file was pretty simple. This was her first time on the radar; at least in this area. Nice of her kids to dump her back home. It was even nicer of their father to suggest to her kids to dump her back home. Everybody was so nice to her lately, even the woman before her. The woman continued to read, while humming to herself. Kate could barely hear it, but it was there, and so was she. The urge to go to the bathroom had returned, but again the humming, yellow haired, fat lady had read her file through and now was on a second go round. Kate couldn't decide if she was pondering an argument she had with her husband last night or taking mental notes for a grocery list. Definitely the husband thing Kate decided, the bee-hived woman probably went off on a humming tangent and spoiled dinner. If Kate wasn't so uncomfortable she'd almost feel sorry for her, after all that meant the woman was married.

Kate could distract herself no longer. "Excuse me... is there a restroom around here?"

Bee-hive woman looked up from her third attempt at reading the file and gave her a puzzled look.

"You want to go to the restroom? I don't think I can..." the woman began.

Kate shot the woman a look that either scared her or promised to because the plump little woman jumped up from her chair and lead Kate to a small closeted space in an inner office. As Kate threw up the back of her robe and shucked her jeans, she immediately slammed the door. The wooden door thumped loudly banging back into Kate's face. She found, upon quick inspection, the middle-aged woman's plump little size five wedged in between the door and the frame.

Kate yelled out of anger and disbelief, "What the hell do you think you're doing, you stupid bitch!" Kate released pent up anger towards the clerk. She avoided many a patient and staff member during her brief incarceration at the hospital. She knew very well a display of anger added time. She also knew instinctively she was not in control of anything let alone her hidden rage.

Yellow bee-hive lady wedged her foot even deeper against Kate's drag.

"Look here, Missy, I am not having any suicides on my watch. This is my office and this is how I run it. As for you, remember you are new here. To my mind you have nowhere else to go but here. I'll tell you right here and now you better mind your p's and q's or you could be here for a long time."

Kate heard the speech. It wasn't the first time she'd heard "The Speech" Every time she heard it she hoped it was the last time. "The Speech" made her feel less than she had felt at twelve or ten or even eight. She had shouldered heavy responsibilities at a young age. Somehow ever since she hit forty, she had gone back in time. This time was not unlike the first time. Those who gave "The Speech" reminded her that she had no choice. She was less. The anger burned brighter with every recital she encountered.

Somehow the plump little lady knew she had touched a nerve. She didn't know how, but she'd been around enough of "those people" as she chose to call them at least have an inkling when "they" were riled.

"My name is Glenda and you are Kate. Is that right?" The bee-hive lady queried.

The little yellow bee-hive lady removed her glasses and let them hang by their sparkly chain. Glenda looked into the still sitting Kate's eyes and smiled a little pearly toothed smile.

"I hope we didn't get off on the wrong foot, Kate. Are you finished yet? I'll stand just around the corner and let you finish. Then we can sit together and fill out your forms. How does that sound?"

Glenda kept her voice light and a bit sing-songy.

Kate felt that Glenda may have laid it on a little too thick. She thought to herself, "For Christ's sake if I was going to off myself, I would have taken care of that little bit of business at home." She knew, but didn't care that the woman was jumpy being alone with a crazy person. Again, Kate thought the woman might be on the wrong career path.

Kate walked peacefully to her chair. Glenda sat back behind her desk. She read through the various documents and asked Kate the particulars. Date of birth, marital status, children and their ages, employment history, education background. Kate answered almost each inquiry truthfully, but all calmly. Glenda felt a little more at ease. The information she gathered from the woman wasn't the norm for someone her age. Kate did in fact start her life running. She had accomplished a lot with what she was given. Marital status: divorced, children: 2 girls ages 19 and 18 Education: advanced...who cares?

Kate had been asked these questions so many times over the years that she literally responded absent of thought. What did it matter anymore? She had lost herself over the years and everything else. Kate guessed Glenda asked her last question, and then there was something about some guy taking her to her dorm. It didn't matter. She would wait. She knew going most of the day without food or cigarettes would allow her to sleep easily again.

"Kate, I'm going to run a few copies of this in the hall. Will you be alright here?" Glenda began to point to the hallway that held the restroom. Kate was already balancing her chin in her hand on the arm of the chair. Kate nodded her head yes and closed her eyes.

NEW DIGS

Kate shifted in the office chair. Although sleeping her hand felt numb. Her head teetered on her hand and then suddenly dipped toward her lap. Kate caught herself by grabbing both arms of the chair. She gasped and her eyes flew open. A small, seemingly ageless man sat before her. No plump yellow bee-hive Glenda, but someone who seemed to be straight out of a Rocky and Bullwinkle cartoon. The man didn't speak, he didn't move, he just sat as if waiting.

Glenda walked in as Kate found herself under Percy's scrutiny. Percy was studying the new resident. He was respectful if more than slightly curious.

"Is this the famous car thief, railway walker and water bomber?"

Kate nodded yes and then chuckled almost inaudibly. Glenda stood close behind Percy and whispered in his ear. Kate caught what she thought was asshole driver and no transports.

"Glenda is going to lunch. She has left it to me to get you checked into your dorm. I hope you don't mind?"

Kate stood at the mention of a dorm and grabbed her little bag along with the huge brown bear she refused to leave behind.

Percy stood in kind and continued, "Your dorm is located on the other side of the campus. I think you'll be comfortable there. We have a few that have been updated. Yours is one of them."

He led her out of the green door and locked it behind him. He hung a sign on the door, but Kate wasn't interested in anything but getting on with it.

"Kate, we're taking this red truck here." He pointed to an older model Chevy parked near the door. Kate opened a creaky door and sat her stuff on the seat between them.

Percy kicked in the engine and slowly commanded the cruiser down a winding drive. As the truck crested the hill Kate could see a tree cluster. Inside the surround of trees, she saw a low brick wall darkened, as if by fire, and crumbling toward the interior. Beyond the small forest loomed a compound of assorted yellow brick buildings with glass door fronts connected by concrete sidewalks.

Kate had felt anxious during the short ride to the dorm so she asked Percy to share his story to calm her mood. She found his experiences at Brown ran the gamut. He worked as a technician, or what he preferred to call an attendant, right out of high school. He attended nursing school during the days while he safeguarded the dorms at night until he was hired on as a psychiatric nurse. A few years earlier, he decided he'd had enough of the tumultuous life of a head nurse and retired to the easy life of admission clerk. He kept his hand in the dorms, which left him able to spend the bulk of his days managing the farm his parents had left after their passing.

As Percy eased the truck into a space marked reserved in front a honey brick building, Kate suddenly threw out, "You know Percy, I bet you can take down the big'uns, huh?"

Percy immediately shot back, "Yep, the big'uns are easy. It's the scrappy little ones like you that are challenging."

Kate ripped her eyes of the dorm and looked straight into the smiling eyes that waited. She felt her eyes smile back.

 Kate quickly surveyed her new residence. It was one story with only two ways out that she could see. Inside were people milling around. There were people wearing scrubs at the counter. A long counter dominated the front area of the building and three couches flanked the walls of an adjacent room. The couches were occupied with people wearing street clothes.

Kate did not hear the engine shut off. She was too involved in her study. Before she knew it, Percy was standing at her door. "Hey Kate, time to go in." he started. He didn't know if she would bolt or be compliant, but he was ready for anything. Experience taught him this transition was normally the most difficult one.

Kate grabbed her things and swung down through the open the door. Percy guided his charge to glass double doors. Once there he stopped and swung a card on a chain out of his shirt and swiped it through a card reader that jutted out of the frame of the door. The door clicked and they stepped through to the threshold of Kate's new home. Staff and patients alike swung their heads up in unison to see the new resident. Percy led Kate to the counter. A pretty young woman stepped up to the counter and smiled warmly at Kate.

"Hi!" She greeted Kate cheerfully.

The woman paused mid chirp to look down at the paper Percy placed in her outstretched hand.

"We've been expecting you. I'll show you your room in a few minutes, but first we need to check you in."

Percy looked at Kate to reassure himself that she would do alright at least this first night.

"Michelle, I need to get back to the office, so if you think you've got it, I'll be on my way."

Michelle studied Kate for a minute. Kate appeared calm, no shaking, no aggressive stance, and yet not quite what she expected from the report she read earlier. Michelle responded, "Yeah, we're doing fine right now. I'll let you know, ok?"

Kate stood transfixed at the counter. In the distance she heard an engine start and move slowly away. Next, she heard Michelle's voice coax her to the hospital scale that stood against the wall. Kate inwardly groaned. Her new warden toted down her weight on a clipboard and led her through the requisite blood pressure and temperature check. Once Michelle had fulfilled the physical health requirements, she announced it was time to see her room.

Kate followed the smiley blonde woman down a long hall and through an open door. The décor was "mod mental patient" downplayed. A large window separated her from the outside world. As open as the window made the room, it showed its new occupant that she was indeed shut in. A quick peruse of the of the edges of the glass proved there was no opening it, the only opening in this room was out to the so called dormitory, which, Kate was informed, was to would be open at all times unless at night and that was for safety purposes only. Two twin beds occupied most of the room. Smiley Michelle smiled even more when she announced to Kate that she would have her own room and therefore her choice of beds.

"Yay," Kate muttered under her breath.

Michelle's smile dampened a little, but without missing a beat, the lovely Michelle held the best for last. The pink clad nurse stepped over to a door at the end of the room. She held out a key to Kate. "This is your closet. Remember to keep it locked at all times. Other residents might want what you have and you are the only person who will prevent them from getting it."

After the end of the required speech, Michelle looked directly in Kate's eyes.

Michelle mouthed very slowly, "People steal."

Without missing a beat, the sweet blonde haired nurse audibly ended her speech.

"If you need anything, just go to the counter and we will help you."

Kate blinked and the room was empty except for the new female resident and a brown fluffy bear.

A few minutes later, Kate stretched out on the gold carpeted floor in the Women's Day Room. It wasn't hard for her to find. She stepped out of her room and voila! As for unpacking, she took the suitcase and put it in the closet. It seemed more than ridiculous to her that she should take time out to put her five articles of clothing into the chest of drawers. She didn't have a lot in her wardrobe. She reasoned it would be more embarrassing to have to wear clothes from the donated clothes bin once her own disappeared.

That is one lesson she had learned during her first "*vacay*." Kate did take time to line her beauty products up on the tall shelf in her closet. The display was for her alone. It would be a daily reminder that even though her family didn't know how, they still did care. Stuff was stuff, you didn't want to seem like you had too little or too much, because "any attention was unwanted attention". Anyone or anything could stand in your way from sleeping in a room with a sealed window as opposed to one you can open.

Kate had been able to get comfortable in the day room. She found a use for the bear. He was soft enough that she was able to rest her head on his stomach. This way she was able to cushion her neck while elevating her eyes to the right height to watch the television which dominated the small room. Since she had been there, the tape on the music videos rolled at least three times. She didn't question her need. It was just something she did when the switch flipped. That and drive, but Kate's last drive put her back in the hospital. She guessed maybe someone got wise.

All she had was country music now. It was calming and peaceful. She was bone weary from months of constant agitation and little sleep. Right here, right now, she could focus on the music and hopefully rest. The dorm was quiet.

She wasn't allowed to go out on the grounds without staff escort. Every facility had its own rules. This particular one had a step up program like most did. The first three days the "resident" had to be escorted everywhere. The second three days, you were allowed to be let out with a group. And then if you minded yourself and show that you were responsible, you'd be allowed to go out on your own. She understood the reasoning. Yes, it would be nice to go outside. Once it would have mattered a great deal to her, but at this stage one week in comparison to being confined for months on end wasn't much. They let her out to smoke a couple times a day. So, she reasoned, the promise of being outside, even with an escort, was better than being locked up without hope of freedom. She knew convicts who were treated better. Comfort and quiet weren't bad even when forced upon you. "Besides," Kate thought, "it's too damn cold out there right now."

The videos rolled. Kate watched a skinny, heavily made-up blonde country singer standing on a sand dune, with the breeze blowing her many scarves behind her. The sound coming from the TV was low. Kate listened to the music as it lightly filled her ears. She began to picture the words in her mind. Kate felt herself relax as the music wafted over. She shut her eyes and drifted.

"Ha ha ha ha!"

Kate snapped her head up as a laugh track boomed, bouncing annoying chuckles through the room that was meditatively peaceful moments earlier. Kate jumped to her feet to find a large, black curly black-haired woman standing over her with the remote control in a huge pasty hand.

"What the fu..?!" Kate's voice trailed as she realized that not only was this a young woman but she was also twice her size. From the look on Kate's challenger's face, she was observing Kate. The young woman studied her keenly sizing up her opponent. Kate knew nothing about the burly young challenger. Kate also knew instinctively that if she did not establish herself, she would not be watching any more country videos or television at any rate.

Kate began very loudly, "I was watching that!"

Kate purposely ignored the glaring factors that weighed in on the confrontation. It did not matter that to Kate that her opponent had eight inches on her and, to Kate's mind, at least sixty pounds.

"Well, I'm back bitch and this is my TV!" Kate's challenger established her dominance loudly.

Kate kicked the bear out of the reach of the woman looming overhead while taking the opportunity to distract her and stand without losing her advantage.

"Well, that's just too damn bad. I was here first!"

Kate stood as tall as her five feet could get her. She met the woman decibel for decibel all the while staring fiercely into the glaring muddy brown eyes.

Kate had begun the argument, but the longer she talked, the angrier she became. Kate's opponent had started off angry, but quiet.

Kate amped up the volume, "Give me the fucking remote bitch, you took it from me and I was here first."

The brunette's face was now red, her dark curls stuck to her large skull.

A tall thin man dressed in scrubs drawn in from the outer room quickly took a position between the two contenders and said, "Now, Janice, she was here first. You know the rules. Give me the remote and get your things ready; we have to go to the hospital tonight."

Janice puffed her face up as if to respond, but the orderly glared at her. She placed the remote in his hand without looking at him. Kate noticed the large hand shaking as it surrendered the valuable prize. The orderly placed the black sleek box in Kate's calm hand.

"Git on now," he ordered.

Janice stomped down the hall. The orderly Steve, as it said on his name tag, looked straight into Kate's eyes and said, "I heard the scuffle clear at the desk. You need to take care around here. You did the right thing, but you take care."

His eyes scanned the day room and then, "Did you see a pen lying around here?"

Kate shook her head no.

"We came up one short at the desk. We're missing a pen, if you see it let me know. Some people swallow things, probably find it in the x-rays tonight…" he mumbled.

Then Kate heard him mumble something else. It sounded a little like "Fucking crazy ass bitch." Kate resumed her position, head on bear, prone in front of the glowing picture. The orderly continued to swear under his breath as he walked away.

"Woo hoo, Kate is it?" A grandmotherly type woman sat on the floor by her.

"I have a few things for you," she said to Kate.

Kate shifted her weight and brought herself up to a sitting position.

"Yes, I'm Kate, and you are?" Kate peered at the name tag that said Betty R.N. "Betty."

The woman was small like Kate but had short gray and black hair. She seemed nice enough, but it's easy to be nice when you have a key that will let you out after eight hours. Betty's face was patient. She waited for the new girl to accept her presence and then started once again.

"Now, I brought your dinner from the dining hall. Tuesday, you will be expected to go with the other residents. You came here without a coat, but I have one here that was donated by a local merchant. Don't worry. It's new. It's not much, but it will keep you warm. I also have a pair of shoes for you, because we also noticed that you only have your slippers. You will have to wear something more functional outside."

Betty brought forth a bag from which she first brought out a purple fiber filled coat. Kate felt indignity rise in her throat.

"Now let's try it on." Betty held the coat up for Kate.

Kate slowly put the coat on. She tried not to look at it. She immediately gave up praises for the lack of a mirror in the room. It did indeed fit, of course it did.

The shoes were next. Kate held her breathe hoping against all hope while Nurse Betty slowly placed the shoebox before Kate. She had thrown her own tennis shoes off at her Mom's house because they had no laces. They couldn't take her laces here because she had no shoes. So, what did they do? Kate opened the box and saw two bright white tennis shoes; no laces here: Velcro.

Betty insisted she sit on the loveseat in the corner and try on the tale tell-tale gear. "Well," Kate thought to herself, "if I don't look crazy now, I'm sure they have a pair of red sweats to add to the ensemble." Kate sat with her head down studying the new shoes. Her self-appointed elf took a seat beside her. Kate's gaze switched from the bright white geriatric gear to a warm brown leather clog with low wooden heels. She suddenly felt shoe envy.

"Hey, Betty? Where'd you get those shoes?" It was out. She couldn't take it back even if she wanted to. She wanted those shoes.

"Oh, I got them at the discount store. They weren't very expensive, but they are really comfortable."

"Wanna trade?"

"No, I like them fine plus it's not allowed either. If you do well, you'll be able to go on an outing soon. I'm sure they will have them for quite some time, ok? Now, you need to eat. You have a smoke break at nine then meds, then it's lights out."

Nurse Betty motioned to the plastic bag sitting on the table, "I'll see you at med time."

Kate stretched her little frame against the light brown floor. She wasn't in a hurry to eat. The hunger pangs had long since vanished. She guessed pizza wasn't on the menu here or it was a special treat used to keep the patients in line. The Styrofoam container sat on the white linoleum table but no smell came from it. More than likely she thought the food froze from the trip through the bitter wind. She did pick up a hint of coffee though. The odor turned her stomach.

She wondered how many pots she had made over the years. No matter what, she never succumbed to the wonder drink. Grandma's Sanka had once tempted her, but it was more the heavy spoonful of sugar and the deliberate pour of milk that had done the trick. Kate remembered the bitter through the soft and sweet. It never tempted her again. She walked hesitantly across the quiet floor and sat down on the metal chair.

With very little anticipation she uncovered her meal. Kate had begun long ago to expect very little and the meal that lay before her was that indeed. A cold biscuit stared up at her. In the second divider lay something grayish green. The third divider was empty. Kate found the meal order taped to the lid. Experience had taught her in situations like this it was always important to check the menu so you a least had a clue of what you were eating. The white paper read Vegetarian Meal: Biscuit and sautéed spinach. Kate saw a biscuit. That wasn't difficult, but spinach?

Kate grabbed the Styrofoam cup and walked into the nearby bathroom where she poured out the coffee and thoroughly washed and rinsed the disposable container while thinking that the vegetarian diet would not work at this institution. She filled the cup with water from the bathroom sink and carried it to the table. She settled herself once more before the meal. Kate found herself very happy that her stomach jumped at the sight of food. After all, she reminded herself, hunger is the best sauce.

Smiley Nurse poked her head around the corner into the day room. Kate had long since finished her state-appropriated feast. She was soaking in the rays of "If you think I'm Country." She discovered that the video station had put two more videos into the loop. One was a somber ballad about the journey a man takes from childhood to old age. Kate judged it thought-provoking, at best. She found the other new video enjoyable, almost funny. It featured a "good ole boy" in an awkward situation where he fumbles to save face, and finally throws his hands up and walks off camera. Just as the run looped to begin again, she heard.

"Kate? If you want to smoke, you'll have to go now!" Betty called.

Kate quickly jumped up and almost ran to her room. The key clicked in the closet door lock revealing her untouched suitcase. Frantically, she fished around in the back until she came up with the rectangular pack and the black lighter sticking out of the open end. Kate cinched up the flannel robe around her waist and made her way to the glass door in the front of the building.

Kate had very little idea of the number of residents on the floor. During the day there was a constant movement of people in and out. Tonight, just at a glance Kate speculated that there were about maybe fifteen people waiting patiently for their last chance to self-medicate before the door was locked for the night. Two male orderlies stood by the waiting line. The orderly that stood at the end of the line was an older man. His head was bald and he had a big graying handle bar mustache. Kate could hear him even before she could see him.

The other orderly was a young man. He was thin and tall. She recognized him from her earlier confrontation. He would have been attractive if he had not been so thin. She studied him for a minute and decided he might be close to the age of her oldest daughter. She thought, if she got a chance, she would ask him.

The too loud, too happy attendant that stood at the end of the line scanned Kate briefly. "You'll have to put a coat on and some shoes if you want to go out." He informed her, "Can't go out in night clothes!"

Kate turned on a dime.

"You need to hurry if you're going out. We don't have much time!" Kate could hear the orderly boom as she rushed down the hall.

Kate decided to call him Walrus. In the past two years, Kate had met a lot of professional health care workers. She found that sure they were there to help whoever, but more importantly they were there to enforce the rules. She had given up trying to befriend anyone that she shared a room, a dorm or any facility with. It never helped in the long run. She internalized her lessons: mind yourself, follow the rules, keep your eye on the prize and dodge all the seen and unseen bullets along the way.

Kate threw the bathrobe on the bed. Then she kicked the soft black house shoes off. She unlocked her closet again. While standing she shoved her bare feet in the stiff white geriatric shoes and grabbed the purple coat. Hurriedly, she crossed the dorm back to the entrance pulling the purple plastic smelling coat on while standing short of the locked glass door.

The Walrus saw Kate approach the door from the front patio. He moved through the huddle of patients to slide his key card through the slot. He was a little slower than Kate would have like, but she reasoned that if she didn't have patience at this point in the game she hadn't learned anything.

Kate knew it wasn't just the addiction to tobacco that held a hold on her, but choice. Smoking was more than a distasteful health risk, but it was freedom. It was the ability to go outside even though you were step-one. It was a break in the monotony of a long uneventful day. Most of all it was the chance to be with people who might have a smile or even a story to share because they felt a little easier, a little freer, and maybe even, outside on a cold patio at 9:00 at night in a freezing Kansas wasteland, a little closer to home.

Kate fished about for her cigarettes in the pocket of her coat. She reached in one pocket and then the other. Both times she came up empty. Kate knew after the first pocket, the crew on the patio was watching her progress. Yet, when she came up empty handed, the crew looked elsewhere. Kate stuck both of her hands in her pockets and stood silently surrounded by a cloud of second hand smoke. She had resigned herself to enjoying her first fifteen minutes of relative freedom in a very long time.

As she gazed off into the darkness of acres and acres of frozen farmland, Kate felt a nudge on her right shoulder. When she turned she saw a figure in a blue down padded coat with a stocking cap pulled down low over his forehead. A big red nose protruded. The figure pushed his hand into her side. Without making too much movement Kate saw a cigarette and lighter positioned close to her pocket. Sliding her right hand out of the pocket, she soundlessly accepted the gift without touching the hand that offered it. Kate swung the prize up to her lips and flicked the blue lighter.

Kate deftly placed the lighter in the crook of the giver's left hand, nodded a thank you to the dark figure that was already edging itself closer to the other side of group. The men in the center huddled, spit and talked while taking long slow drags. The Walrus and Thin Man smiled and exchanged small talk with other patients standing on the cold concrete. Most of the patients Kate saw them talking to throughout the day were women. Since there were very few women smoking, their conversations were limited to their children and their jobs. Kate listened closely to glean a little from their shop talk as far as diagnosis or commitments but there were none. Disappointed, Kate just looked at the stars in the blue black sky and was grateful.

"OK guys, it's time to put 'em out and get inside. I'm 'bout to freeze my butt off!" Walrus proclaimed.

Thin Man did the key card trick and both men held the doors open. The huddle of men in the center of the yard birds obediently crushed the burning embers and dutifully filed into the well-lit building. The smokers on the outer edges of the patio shuffled their feet and a few of the orbiters took the opportunity to light up once more. These brave souls stretched the break to flex whatever little time they could find to pretend, if only for a moment, that they could bend and change rules to fit their own desires. Even so, these few rebels kept their eye on the line snubbing out their silent burning protest in time to fall behind as soon as space was made apparent.

And Kate? Kate had no choice at this time. She was still new and thus closely watched. She was sure to hold one door while Thin Man held the other. The fifteen minutes that she had spent out in the cold crisp air had been rejuvenating. She felt refreshed and more clearheaded than she had for a while. When the last patient stepped through the threshold, the thin man motioned her to follow. Kate pulled the door with her as she stepped inward and then, out of reflex more than curiosity, she caught her reflection in the glass of the open door. The little bit of freedom she had recaptured only seconds ago disappeared when she found a smallish, female mental patient in an overly bright royal purple coat and equally horribly blinding white shoes staring back at her.

The warm air of the large room hit Kate as soon as she reentered the building. Her fingers tingled as they turned from numb to warm. Kate hurriedly shed the coat and started toward her room.

Walrus stopped her short. "Hey little missy … wrong way."

He smiled and pointed to the line which now included more than just smokers.

"You need to get in line. It's med time, girl!"

Kate stopped in her tracks, reversed and took her place at the end of the line that snaked around the business part of the common room. One by one, each person stepped up to the glass window. They gave their name to the nice Nurse Betty. She disappeared for a minute, returning with two small plastic cups. In turn the patient took whatever the nurse handed them, swallowing the contents of one and chasing it with the other. After which the patient then opened his or her mouth and Nurse Betty inspected the contents. The line ran smoothly, but with the number of patients it was not as fast as Kate would have liked.

For once, Kate found herself wishing for someone to talk to. She almost wished that she knew a few of the residents to pass the time. But then, she reasoned she had no pressing engagements and nothing before her but time. Kate inched closer to the window. She tried not to watch the clock. In the end it became more of a game. The average patient took 3 minutes, five tops if they required a lot of meds. Kate noticed that Percy from admitting appeared as if out of nowhere to watch over the process.

A woman approached the window. Kate had not seen her before. She had not been with the smokers. Kate had not seen her in the day room, or even the women's hall. There she was as big as life and Kate was being generous. The woman had a mop of curly gray hair that hung over her eyes. She wore an overly large green sweater adorned with an array of paper flowers which covered baggy blue sweats.

The woman approached the window mumbling lowly. When Nurse Betty put the cups on the counter before her, she began yelling unintelligibly. The nurse tried to calm the woman, but she wouldn't be calmed. Percy stepped up to the counter, took the cups then led the woman to a nearby couch. He sat by her speaking softly while encouraging her to take the medication. The woman finally relented to Percy's prodding, brought a cup to her mouth and then followed with the second. Percy looked in her open mouth and seemed satisfied. He patted the woman's hand and walked back to the counter.

Kate watched in slight amusement as the woman walked to a trash can not visible to the staff. The woman looked around cautiously and then spit. She immediately scanned the room and focused sharply on Kate. The woman raised a clenched fist in Kate's direction. Kate stood stalk still as the menacing character beamed and gifted Kate with the amazing toothless smile Kate had ever seen.

Kate stepped up to the counter. Nurse Betty smiled almost knowingly. Kate was unsure if she had seen the exchange between her and the other woman. Kate certainly wasn't going to enlighten her.

"Can you give me your name dear?" Betty put the question forth.

In response she mumbled, "Kate Beckenshire."

Nurse Betty nodded approvingly. Kate reached for a cup with three hospital bands clumped together on her forearm.

"Child," said Nurse Betty almost sadly, "why do you have so many bands on your arm?"

Kate shrugged her shoulders and squinted at the white plastic on her wrist, "I guess things just start running together after a while."

The older woman picked through the bands and settled on one. She focused on the writing on the band, Nurse Betty then ran her finger down the sheet of paper lying on the counter. Kate stood waiting patiently.

The nurse reappeared at the window with two small cups as she handed the first to Kate she instructed, "Now, Kate I want you to drink this. It's Haldol. It will taste terrible, but don't worry. I have some lemonade right here that will kill the taste. You will only have to take this for a few days and then after you see the doctor we'll switch to something else."

Kate looked straight into Betty's eyes for the first time. Nurse Betty looked straight back. This right here was the business end of the deal. In the course of her road to Mental Health, Kate had been injected, isolated, over medicated, misdiagnosed and thoroughly mistreated. She knew that because she was legally unable to make her own decisions, any refusal of treatment, whether effective or ineffective, was not a choice for her.

For Betty it was simply a trust issue. The residents should trust that she would keep them from harm. For Kate, it was another reminder that she was less. Yes, she always took the medication. And yet nothing changed. One very dark night she took the whole bottle of medication and upon waking the next morning, was thoroughly pissed...nothing. For Kate there seemed no answer, but to follow orders.

Kate took the plastic cup from the outstretched hand. She brought the medication to her lips and hesitated. She swallowed the bitter vile potion and blindly grabbed for the chaser. The lemonade was almost as horrible as the first round. Once she swallowed the yellow stuff, a shockingly sweet taste settled on her tongue and took the edge off whatever foul concoction the nurse had passively forced on her.

"That was pretty bad wasn't it, Kate?" Kate was surprised by her empathy but then she had nurses use that on her before.

"Yeah, right before a medically induced hibernation or some horrible side effect, with the reminder of refusal means added time." Kate mused to herself.

"Kate? Can you stay here just a minute longer?" Nurse Betty continued, "I want to get some scissors and cut the bands off your arm, if you don't mind?"

Kate waited while the rest of the residents seem to be winding down. Lights were out at eleven. She thought the she might want to catch one more loop if possible. Betty was taking a while fetching the scissors but Kate would lay odds that they probably show up in her television bouncer's film.

"Hey Kate, no luck finding the scissors tonight, but we get the bands taken care of tomorrow, OK?" Nurse Betty patted Kate's arm.

Kate nodded as she mentally steeled herself for the effect of the cocktail. She had many "vacations" over the last four years. She did not remember her doctors' names nor did she remember all the medications that she had been injected with or had ingested on their orders. She did however remember each and every side effect. With a new placement she knew she would once again begin another regimen.

Kate knew very well how difficult it is to take medication especially if you are "mentally ill." She knew after all her adventures with psychotropic medication that she in fact was "crazy." Sure she'd had periods of stability. And she took her medications religiously. Those periods also ended abruptly without warning. Even so, Kate endured: tremors, excessive weight gain, hair loss, difficulty breathing, unconsciousness and even her special favorite "drite in die buksa" to use her father's phrase.

She carried a mental list of hopes followed by another of disappointment. Since her first home dose of Xyprexa, Kate saw a mental warning on her meds: if you are taking this medication you are mentally ill. You will be treated differently by everyone you know and more so by those you don't know.

"Hey Kate... Goodnight."

Nurse Betty was still hanging in as Kate checked her breathing. She reminded herself "in and out" after a several minutes of deep breaths she acknowledged Betty's pleasantry with her own, "Dobreo vecher."

Kate watched the puzzled woman walk away.

Kate was done with the day and walked straight to her room. She couldn't remember the last time she had brushed her teeth. She grabbed the key that dangled between her breasts, leaned over to turn it in the lock on her closet door. A search through the bag showed no toothbrush and no toothpaste.

"Mother fucker!" Kate swore under her breath.

She started for the desk down the hall and then stopped short at the sight of the purple coat lying on her bed. Feeling the weight of the day settle heavily on her shoulders, she entered the closet once more. Tonight she would skip brushing her teeth. She ripped back the Velcro of her sneakers and kicked the shoes across the closet floor. She removed the beloved plaid robe from a hanger and cinched it warmly over her t-shirt and jeans. She dove once again into the mostly empty bag and this time found a pair of rolled up anklets.

To guard her precious few belongings she locked the closet door and tried the knob just in case. She stepped into her private cold room. The windows shone black reflecting the cold winter night. They were as deceptive as a new acquaintance. True, they allowed a patient to feel that the world was just outside. Unfortunately for Kate, tonight the world was a cold dark plain. The darkness and the cold passed through the window and was just as a much a resident in the room as Kate.

LISTEN

"Excuse me, Kate?" Smiley Blonde Nurse inquired of the sleeping Kate. Kate peeked her head out from underneath her requested extra blanket. Kate found earlier that sleeping beneath the sheets was like sleeping in an ice tray. The cold seeped through them like water. She spent the night fully dressed, wrapped in her housecoat, huddled under the state issued tan blanket. Sleep had not come easy in her new abode, but then it had not come easy for the last several years. At night, she lay wrapped up against the cold waiting for warmth to set in. She had learned to lie motionless willing her limbs and trunk to relax, waiting for rest, which came unwillingly. This morning Nurse Smiley interrupted the dream. For this Kate was grateful. She welcomed waking up to her Miss America face compared to the usual helplessness.

"Kate," The nurse continued, "You will be meeting Dr. Schwarz this morning for a med check. She will be here at 9. You have a half an hour to get ready. You can have breakfast after your appointment. You need to get around, OK?"

"Yes, ma'am." Kate almost met her smile.

Kate threw the blanket back and slid off the bed. The halls were once again empty. She had missed the morning traffic, Kate noted happily. After begging for toiletries, she laid siege to the vacant ladies' room. She set to brushing her teeth, ran a comb through her shoulder length brown hair repeating her mantra. "Someday I'll get out of here. It could be today."

Thirty minutes later, Kate sat outside of the office in the small hallway behind the medication window. She counted four doors. Each door had a placard naming the inhabitant of the office. Doctor Schwartz's door stood closed to her. Nurse Smiley had helped her through the "pre-reqs." The nurse reported a loss of ten pounds and Kate's blood pressure appeared to be border line. Kate remained passive. She was anticipating her meeting with the Doctor. Kate had met quite a few doctors. She evaluated them from seemingly concerned to help, to throwing drugs at her problem damn the results and then on to the next patient.

Suddenly, a heavy woman rushed down the short hall. Her arms were full of bags containing files. The woman grasped the door marked Doctor Schwarz, yanked it open and slammed it shut behind her. Kate tensed in her plastic chair.

The wait could have been long or short, time ceased to have much meaning to Kate. The door opened and the harried woman reappeared.

"You must be Kate. I'm Dr. Schwarz. Please come in and have a seat." The older woman was very specific.

She did not question but read the situation. The office was tiny. The room contained two chairs and a small desk. Dr. Schwarz had unloaded her bagged files and stacked them on the desk. Kate could see her file open on top of the stack.

"Now, let's see here…..yes. You are what we call a frequent flier: three hospitalizations and an outpatient clinic in 40 months. This is your third day with us. We have you on Haldol, which is a liquid antipsychotic. My recommendation is that we put you on Risperdal, an oral antipsychotic, and see how you do."

The doctor's eyes moved from the file to Kate's face. Kate did not flinch.

"Dr. Schwarz, I'm not psychotic, schizo-effective, or even schizophrenic. I'm Bipolar. I have taken Xyprexa, Seroquel, and even Risperdal. For some reason, every doctor I've ever seen has given me an antipsychotic. I have taken them and I'm still stuck in a revolving door. Don't you think something may be wrong with that?"

"Kate, you are not a doctor. There is a reason that your previous doctors have given you anti-psychotics."

"There's a reason that the anti-psychotics don't work," Kate responded.

"What do you suggest?" Doctor Schwarz turned to scan the open file before her.

Kate took the opening, "Lithium."

Before the word had Left Kate's mouth the doctor pounced. "No. Lithium requires lab work. The levels have to be checked regularly. We don't do that here."

Kate held her ground, "You're telling me that you can justify transporting one patient to the university hospital two hundred miles away every two weeks, to make sure they don't have the contents of an office supply store in their stomach, but you can't do a simple one time blood draw? Look, Dr. Schwarz, I know I'm not a Doctor, but I'm tired. I want to be well. I want my family in my life. I have done everything that I am supposed to do and I am still stuck here. I don't want to stay here any longer than I have to. I want to get on with what I have left."

"I do hear you Kate, I do." Dr. Schwarz scribbled a little in the file.

When she finished, she swiveled back to face Kate. Her eyes were guarded, "I will confer with the hospital board on the matter, but until we come to a decision, you will have to take the Risperdal. Will you agree to this?"

"A minor victory is still a victory," Kate reasoned. This was the first doctor out of many that ever considered her thoughts at all. She nodded in agreement with the doctor. Doctor Schwarz scribbled again, this time on a yellow post-it, stuck it on top of Kate's file and reached for the next file on the pile. She stopped midway.

"Hey Kate?"

"Yes?" Kate hand was on the doorknob.

"How do you know about Lithium?" Dr. Schwarz inquired.

"I read things. In between driving all over Hell's half acre and sleeping in front of the TV, I read."

"Hmm. Thanks, Kate." By this time the good doctor was deliberating on different file.

Kate mumbled a good-bye and escaped to her styro-foam surprise box. Doctor Schwarz continued reading the next file oblivious to Kate's departure and to her absence.

Kate chewed thoughtfully on the glazed doughnut that appeared in the white box. She didn't much care for it but ate it anyway. Today was her third day at Brown State Hospital. Soon she would be able have meals with the rest of the dorm. She doubted that the food would improve, but she would be allowed to go out on the buddy system. She didn't really have anyone in mind but she would keep her eye out for someone who would fit the bill.

The residents had long since returned from breakfast from whence they had dispersed to their separate rooms, duties, and activities. Kate felt a little adventurous considering her good fortune during her med check. Her first stop was the nurse's counter. She stood towards the end where the telephone was located. Nurse Smiley was too busy with paperwork to notice Kate waiting patiently at the opposite end of her station.

"Uh huh, she's blonde and a real looker. She's even got pictures of herself with some really famous guys. Come on out and see."

Jim had been polite enough to keep his voice low but he could not contain his excitement.

Kate followed the excited little man to the main room where the male residents huddled around what she guessed was the newest resident. Couches flanked all sides of the room. Kate chose the couch directly opposite of the mass of men. Jim sat beside her. The men who she had seen only move from the couches for meals or to smoke had suddenly become animated and full of life.

With their backs toward Kate, they laughed, and passed something among their little group while jostling for space yet closer to an unseen light. Their language was suddenly clean. The men stood straight and tall. Kate was amused and disgusted at the same time.

Walrus, who had been observing the commotion, checked his watch and called for lunch line up. The covey of males immediately headed toward the back door abandoning the subject of their adoration without thought. From the huddle emerged a woman dressed smartly in black leather. Her feet were encased in black boots with silver buckles at the ankle and again at the knee. Her face was artfully painted and her platinum hair was curled falling loosely around her shoulders. From Kate's vantage point she could not surmise her age, but curiosity drew her closer to the abandoned visitor.

Kate put on her best almost real smile as she approached the stranger.

"Hey," she put forward lightly. "I'm Kate and you are?"

The woman neither acknowledged her attempt at courtesy nor did she move to take Kate's outstretched hand. Kate ignored what would be normally taken as a slight and sat down beside the seemingly waxen figure.

Kate started again. "I'm pretty new here too. This is my second day. I have no earthly idea when I get out either."

"My lawyer is getting me out. He always does. I'm probably leaving soon."

The doll spoke into the air then the shifted a little on the sofa.

"Wow, that's great." At this point Kate had heard so many getting sprung stories she had good reason to doubt the newbie's pronouncement.

"My name is Celia. I'm a model. I've appeared in many commercials and talk shows. I know all kinds of famous people. Would you like to see my pictures?" Celia's voice sounded hollow to Kate.

Kate sensed that this simple speech was well worn. Celia did not offer Kate her infamous pictures, but rather clutched from Kate what she could see were black and white photo copies of pictures. Kate peered intently at the top of the stack. She recognized a very youthful grinning Barbie hugging a talk show host who was popular during Kate's youth.

"Is that you?"

"Yes."

"Have you had dinner? When they come back they will bring us something."

"I'm not hungry. I just took my medication before I left. My attorney will be here soon. He just has to take some funds out for the hospital charges. All my money is tied up in a trust. When he gets it out, he'll come get me."

"O.K. Whatever is best for you." Kate tried to placate her.

Kate stared at the side of Cecelia's face for a while. She tried to study her. Kate peered under the porcelain, up under the facade, but saw nothing. Whoever she was or whatever she was had been vacated a long time ago. Yes, Kate admired her appearance but the woman appeared to be void, absent. Kate knew that just as she had survived this little stretch of whatever it was, somehow Celia may not been able.

Kate's congenial conversation had dried up. She continued to sit with the real live doll simply for lack of anything better to do. Celia sat statuesquely with her finely manicured fingers grasping days long gone.

Walrus accompanied a heavy set man in a dark gray winter Pendleton into the circle of couches. Kate assumed this to be the attorney yet he was different from any lawyer Kate knew. He wasn't shady but sharp. He stood for a moment and then loudly cleared his throat. Celia stood, the "attorney" left, Celia followed. And Kate watched.

Kate sat alone in the couched room. The cold air from the power couple departure swirled around the room and died. She wondered as she gazed into the black early evening. Which of us is worse off; a breathing mannequin who is well cared, but not in any sense living or a cast off who is grasping at some hope of life? Certainly, Kate reasoned, she herself did not possess the beauty or the stature that oozed from Celia's being, but if I'd given up...could that have been me?

MAKE NEW FRIENDS

The woman had long brown hair with beauty shop golden streaks. Kate could not see her face, but her swollen belly drew Kate's attention. A shadow of a man stood by the woman. He had one hand on the woman's shoulder waved Kate away with the other. Kate moved her lips to speak, to beg, to plead her case, but the man would not hear her. The shadow turned toward the pregnant woman. Kate had been dismissed.

A blast of wind jostled Kate awake. It was followed by a shrill whistle. She now consciously listened to the sounds of the early winter day. She didn't open her eyes but rested. It was the dream. It appeared early every morning as she slept. She never expected it but yet it was the only consistent thing in her life. She knew why it appeared and also that it would continue. Yet every morning she lay in bed, fighting off the absence of emotion that reigned in on her daily. It was a reminder of her past and her present. She had tried to run from both only to be caught at her most vulnerable moments.

"Good morning star shine," she thought. Then muttered "fuck it."

People began walking up and down the hall. Kate had held her bladder until she could hold it no longer. She made a mad dash across the hallway into the communal restroom.

"Thank God for stalls." she thought as she slammed the door.

From inside the stall she heard shuffling feet on the tile floor. She was in no mood to go toe to toe with anyone over a mirror or sink. So she sat and counted the weeks since her departure. She knew she had a six week window before her position was filled and she would be put on the inactive roster. That window became smaller with every day that passed. Her ability to support herself would be gone and she would have to start from ground zero for the fourth time. One foot in front of the other she told herself.

The shuffling became faint then absent. Kate swung the blue metal door open. She stopped at one of the three sinks on the blue tiled wall. Kate looked deeply into her own eyes while soaping and washing her hands. The restroom door opened. Kate turned the water off as soon as she heard the stall door shut. Minutes later she was wondering was surprise the white Styrofoam box held this morning.

Once again the inhabitants of the dorm vacated the building. Kate longingly watched her dorm mates leave. This was day three for her. She was left behind under the watchful eyes of the staff. She noticed this morning there were two new members. Well at least they were new to Kate. She knew well to stay away from staff any staff. They would put in their time and then would go on home to their happy families. Kate giggled audibly. She immediately clamped her hands over her mouth.

She checked the two women manning the desk. Neither nurse looked in her direction. "Good," she thought, as they gave no signs of hearing her break her composure. A few notes in her file could lengthen her stay. Plus there would be queries. Kate's plan was to be compliant until she had served her term. She hadn't and wouldn't display her guts for someone to see so they could feel all warm and fuzzy about themselves. So far, it hadn't been a problem, but on smoke break last night she saw Walrus studying her. He was trying to figure something out, but she didn't give him an opening. He can buddy up with others, she thought, and he can use his psyche courses on someone else. She filed that information for future use. The teddy bear waited. CVC began the loop. She watched a lonely cowboy sing.

Kate couldn't decide if the station had snuck in a few more videos while she slept. She surmised that the station had kept her two favorites so she was content. She stretched and relaxed in front of the TV until she heard the back door open. Again, residents walked the long hall. The men crossed through the day room. Kate had learned that the men were not allowed to stay in the room without staff present. From her observations the men seemed to enjoy their own company leaving staff more time to take care of important business.

"Hey, I like that singer. He is really cute." Kate heard a voice come from behind her. She turned her head to find another body perched on the dayroom sofa.

"Hi. I'm Brenda and you are Kate, right?' Kate sat up to face her company. Brenda was a pasty thing. Her thin brown hair parted to show wire rim glasses perched on a sharp pimply nose.

"Yeah, that's right." Brenda studied Kate for a moment.

Her gaze traveled to Kate's shoes. Rule number infinity. Residents must wear shoes while in common areas.

"Wow! I like your shoes. They look new." Brenda continued to stare at Kate's feet.

"Would you like to trade?" Kate suggested.

Without hesitation, Brenda sat closely only the floor beside Kate and peeled off her shoes. Kate tugged at the new Velcro. Within minutes, Brenda was walking around the brown carpet admiring her new acquisition. Kate pulled on the cracked graying substitutes that she now owned. Brenda's shoes were worn which Kate initially liked but after putting them on she found what she didn't like: they were also a little damp and sharply imprinted with her new friend's foot. "Oh well," she thought, "can't go back on it now."

"Gee Kate, thanks for the shoes. I just love them! Whenever you want just come in my room just knock on the door. I have a lot of light."

"Christ," Kate thought to herself, "I traded shoes to be able to go into another woman's room. Uh uh, not me. I'm not going into anyone's room. Especially, not someone who thinks they owe me."

Nurse Betty appeared in the dayroom entrance. "Kate, here is your breakfast." She placed a white plastic bag on the corner table. It was Nurse Betty's turn to stare at her feet.

"Like my shoes? I traded Brenda for hers. Hers were a little beat up. So I thought she could get some good use out of mine."

Nurse Betty studied Kate's face this time. "That was very nice of you to give her your shoes. She was in need of a good pair. Oh and Kate, the kitchen did change your diet restriction. This morning I believe you have scrambled eggs and toast. Don't forget to clean up after yourself."

Kate studied Nurse Betty's face as intently as she was studied. The trade was charitable therefore acceptable. Kate caught the nurse before she left the room. "Excuse me, Betty? When is smoke break?"

Nurse Betty swiveled on her feet to face Kate. "The first is at 8. The next one is at 10. Anything else?"

"Yeah, are you going out?" Kate fished.

The older woman's face softened just a little, "Sure I'll go out. Enjoy your breakfast, Kate," she was gone.

Kate sat at the metal table. From this vantage point on her right she could see down the long hall to the door that was used for meal line up. To her left she could see the staff sitting at the long counter which she called the desk. In front of her she saw the mesmerizing videos roll on.

The Styrofoam container sat directly in front of her. Kate could smell something eggy coming from the white box. Opening the lid, she found a scoop of what appeared to be scrambled eggs. Two triangles of greasy golden white bread lay beside the yellow dome on the pearly white plate container. She took the plastic white fork in her hand. She scooped up a chunk and placed it in her mouth. As she chewed, disappointment registered quickly.

Kate had somehow expected to taste her scrambled eggs.   At home scrambled eggs were beaten until fluffy and cooked in butter. Kate knew she wasn't a remarkable cook, but she did well enough to entertain friends and business associates. Sunday was always reserved for a large breakfast in her household. Kate's children never turned their noses up at the food she served, but now complained that she no longer cooked for them during their visits. Sitting at the empty table before a soulless meal, Kate mourned the absence of her children.

This definitely wasn't haute cuisine or even close to her home cooking. Kate surprised herself by expecting anything more at a state facility. She dug through the plastic baggy inside the large white shopping bag. Her fingers hit the mark. Pepper, and lots of it she found, did wonders for powdered eggs.

The breakfast wasn't much but, Kate felt sated in front of the TV. She checked the clock at the end of each video. The minutes passed slowly. She felt isolated. None of the patients seemed eager to share their experiences let alone a word or two. Most of the women kept to their rooms. The men seemed to congregate in the main room and didn't accept women into their tight circle. Yet, Kate was new. Because of the rules she was not allowed to leave the building. Whereas, it seemed to her, most of everyone else was allowed to come and go as they pleased.

Three loops passed, Kate was well prepared this time. She had a half of a pack of cigarettes and a lighter in her coat pocket waiting in her room. She was positive that they were waiting for her on the bed because she could see her door from where she lay. No one had gone into her room this morning including her. Kate slept in her clothes as cold as it was. She had to call her parents to make sure they sent her some thermal underwear otherwise she wouldn't be sleeping much until spring broke. She sincerely hoped by then she would be out of this place.

Kate showed up fashionably early to the front door. She watched as others signed a paper while passing into the threshold. She stood patiently at the table and scanned the signatures on the paper. None were familiar just as none of the destinations reported were familiar. They read snack shop, rec therapy, and various classes. Kate noticed that group therapy as well as individual counseling sessions were absent from the list.

Gradually, the men traded their seats across the room for a space closer to the door. Only one remained. Occasionally, the loner would lift an empty bottle to his lips. She supposed he was so busy paying tribute on bended knee to the attractive female superstar singers that he had no idea he was alone.

The staff stepped onto the concrete patio followed by the small mob. True to form the cluster of men spoke only among themselves. Kate recognized her benefactor from the night from previous nights by his blue coat. He was an older man. Sixty- something, Kate guessed. He had sad, kind eyes, but kept to himself in the group. The man watched Kate closely as she reached into her coat pocket and pulled out her cigarettes. He seemed to look elsewhere when he was satisfied Kate wasn't without smokes. She lit one while locating herself next to him.

"Here, I owe you one," she said, offering the half-filled pack to him.

"Naw, I got plenty. Kids send me a carton a week. Thanks, though."

"It's ok. Hey, my name's Kate."

"I'm Henry. Folks call me Hank. You new?"

"Yeah, got here a couple days back. Sure is cold."

"Yeah, where you from?" Kate was grateful he kept the exchange going.

"California really, but I'm from here originally. My folks still live here. Quite a homecoming, huh?"

Henry shrugged his shoulders, "Yup, family's family. They think they're lookin' out for ya."

Smoke Break was quickly over. Kate wandered back to the empty day room.TV had lost its hold on Kate. She lay restless on the brown floor. After flipping through all of the available stations a second time she decided to explore the space available to her. Outside the day room she found a pay phone. Kate reasoned that she should call her kids to see if they had made their way back home. She dialed her home number and an operator intercepted the call. Evidently the line was for local calls only. She hung the receiver up with a little too much force.

"Is there a problem, Kate?" Nurse Smiley chirped from the nurse's station.

"Just trying to call home is all." She tried to chirp in return.

"Well, that phone does not take long distance calls, but I have another line that you can you use if you need to."

"Yes, please. I'm trying to call my family."

"Well, go ahead and use it. Remember you have to dial 9 to get out."

"Thank you, I will."

Kate picked up the receiver of the green phone and once again dialed her home number. It rang until she was certain no one would answer and then she heard her oldest daughter say, "Hello?"

"Hey Amanda, it's Mom."

"Hey Mom, you OK?"

"Well, I'm getting by. I just wanted to see if you and your sister made it back ok."

"Yeah, we're fine, Mom."

"You know rent is due soon and so are the other bills."

"Yeah Mom. I've got your check book."

"Well, you have enough in there to pay rent and bills for a while. If there's anything you need it should cover it. Hopefully, I'll be back soon."

"OK, Mom I'll take care of it."

"I love you."

"Love you, bye."

Quickly, the conversation was over. Changing modes she placed a call to her parents.

"Yello." She heard her Father's once strong gruff voice on the line.

"Hi, Dad." She tried to brighten her voice if nothing else.

"Hi, hun. How you feeling?" Kate could read sympathy, and concern at the same time in the few words that he had uttered.

"Not really happy right now, but I'll get by." Kate pushed down the anger and resentment that had dwelled long in her.

"Well, you know we love you and care about you. We're worried about you, hun."

Kate accepted this statement with mixed feelings. Yes, her parents did love her in their own way. Her father's answer to a long crying jag was "Buck up or get a handle on it, hun." Her parents looked at her as their strong willed independent child who would climb back up in the saddle and go on. And she did. She shouldered everything until her shoulder broke. The laugh was that no one was there to help when she fell into the abyss.

"Hey, Dad, I need you guys to send me some things. Amanda will send you some money and I need you to buy me some stuff."

"Let me get your Mom. She can get what you need." Kate was passed off to her Mother.

"Yello?"

"Mom, I need some things."

"Sure sweetheart, what do you need?"

"I need a carton of cigarettes, a bra, two sets of thermal underwear, two pairs of jeans and two long sleeve shirts."

"You want smalls?" her Mom asked.

"Yes, Mom. Can you send them as soon as possible? My last pair of jeans are falling apart, I've worn them for so long and I don't have anything warm to sleep in."

She tried not to sound desperate, but the cold was getting to her and her jeans were shedding their stitching.

"Sure, sweetheart. Don't worry. I'll take care of it."

"Oh, and Mom? I'm sorry that I gave you and Dad a hard time about resending the order. I know you couldn't do that. I didn't mean to make you feel bad."

"Never mind that now, sweetheart, you just get better, OK? I love you and I'll send your things as soon as I can."

"Thanks, Mom. Oh, yeah, can you send me some cash like maybe twenty?"

"Sure can, Hun."

"Love you, bye."

"Bye-bye."

Kate's Mom quickly and generously validated all her request. Kate was sure of her Mother's love even though it only surfaced in times of absence and dire need, she wished it had been so when she was younger but she would take what she could get. Kate new her parents weren't just old school; they were Old World. The sink or swim kind. She had always reasoned that her drive came from that type of upbringing. With her own children, Kate did her best to teach them to mindfully overcome obstacles.

Kate reflected on her last contact with her girls. All she remembered was anger...unadulterated anger. It hurt her heart and her guilt was more than unbearable. The bump in the road had swallowed her whole.

Nurse Betty was sitting at the desk by the time Kate hung the phone up. Kate knew that she had monitored the call. The older woman simply smiled and asked, "How are your folks?"

"Fine, thanks." Kate returned.

She was sure that the nurse was well aware of her first day at Brown when she had called her parents initially threatening to break off any relationship they had if her parents didn't find some way to get her out of the state mental hospital. She had been picked up after bolting from her childhood home. Who else could have done it? After listening to her parents cry and deny any involvement, she could only take them at their word. Both her Mother and her Father swore that they only wanted what was best for her.

"Hey Kate," Nurse Betty called to her in a kind a gentle voice. Kate's eyes focused on Nurse Betty's soft blue ones.

"Yes?" She answered.

"What do you say we go for a walk?"

Kate looked at the nurse questioningly.

"I bet it's been awhile since you went for a walk. I'm staff so you can go with me. The wind has died down and it's not so cold out right now so we can go before everyone gets back. How does that sound?"

Kate managed to mutter "Good."

Kate scurried off to get her fluorescent coat. She zipped and snapped on the return trip to the desk and stood silently at attention while waiting for the nurse to be relieved of her duty.

Nurse Betty disappeared and returned in a navy blue pea coat with a colorful cashmere scarf. Any time before, Kate would have been envious of her caretakers dress, but now, right now, she was going outside. Kate was full of excitement and anticipation.

The women stepped out of the darkened lobby of the dormitory into a bright brisk winter afternoon. A cool breeze brought the promise of fallow fields and sleeping wild flowers in the surrounding grounds. Before her, the buildings stood erect in the sunshine. The nurse walked through the compound as Kate strolled leisurely behind her. The couple followed the concrete walk to the black asphalt road that Kate had traveled only days before. The older woman stopped, casually waiting for Kate to join her.

"I know you've only been here a few days, Kate. Pretty soon you'll probably think I'm on duty all the time. That's because I am. I officially retired three years ago, but I got so sick of my own company that I went back to work."

Kay caught Betty's profile, "No kids, grandkids?"

"No, I had a couple husbands, but no one ever stuck. Anyway, I enjoy my life. I live according to my own wishes."

Kate smiled and nodded.

"Now Kate, in a few days you'll have more privileges and I want to you to know the boundaries. You can walk anywhere you want with on the grounds with staff. Once you step on this road, however, you can only go where you can be seen by staff from the windows of our building. You belong to one part of the hospital but we also have a section that is for prisoners. You will know them because they wear bright orange jumpsuits. Occasionally, you will see one or two working around the dormitory. Most of the time, you will see them together on campus. They are separate from you. Do you understand?"

"Yes, Ma'am." She would stay separate but she doubted that they were any more dangerous than her dorm mates.

"There is one thing I want to show you though. It's this way."

Kate watched as the bundled blue figure walked toward the southern section of the grounds. She followed close on her trail. They soon came to a brushy wooded area. The foliage was dead now but Kate could tell by the cluster of trees that it would be magnificent in the spring. She wiped out the thought of seeing it herself.

"Kate, come here." Kate shook off the feeling of dread.

She followed the dirt path that Betty traveled ahead of her.

"This is what used to be Brown State Hospital, my dear." Betty said in a voice mixed with awe overridden by remorse.

Kate looked before her guide at a large expanse of red bricks in a mass of rubble. Here and there a hint of wall stood covered by dead choke weed. Further on, lay the skeleton of what appeared to Kate of a building. The crumbling walls were composed of the same rusty material lying on the ground.

"What do you think dear?" Betty asked.

"I think it's a mess." Kate replied.

"We've come a long way since this building was used. We have better drugs and a more therapeutic approach since then. I wanted to show it to you before you started hearing the ghost stories about it. I'm sure the people that were here are long gone. I believe they have found peace at last. Anyway, there it is. It's nothing to fear."

"It's very pretty here." Kate offered

"Yes, it is. Are you ready to go back? Smoke break time before the evening meal you know."

"Yes, Ma'am!" Kate threw a look over shoulder at the rubble of the old hospital and followed her guide toward the new.

The evening passed quickly now that Hank had become her smoke buddy. He always managed to smoke three to her one. They didn't talk much other than discuss his growing extended family. Hank, like Kate, had been "born and raised in Kansas." There was something about small Midwestern towns. They didn't know the same people, but they knew the same people. Walrus was on duty this time. He was working the crowd as usual which was fine with Kate, so long as he didn't work her. She was keeping her guts intact, thank you very much. Dinner was forgettable. For the rest of the dorm it was a social meal, for Kate it was tasteless lumps only recognizable by the menu listing delivered in a bag.

Kate hoped that the dining hall served a better offering. For Kate, med time held more promise of a break in the monotony. And of course she anticipated one character in particular. Tonight the chubby woman wore a brightly knitted sweater covered with multi-colored birds. The woman spoke to no one. She kept up with the line by staring at the feet in front of her. Kate found her forty five minute wait worth every second. The staff tonight was new to her but thoroughly entertaining. Bella, as Kate had named her, stepped up to the counter. The exceptionally young nurse greeted Bella and asked her name. Bella just stood in front of the nurse, head cast downward. The obviously inexperienced young woman began to sign to her. The nurse's hands haltingly went through, "What is your name?" Bella was unresponsive. Clearly frustrated, the woman verbalized the question once more, "Name, please?" Bella stared at the wall behind her red faced inquisitor. The nurse this time sought help. "Brie, this one won't give me her name. What do I do?"

"Show her the list," answered a voice from the back.

The young nurse showed Bella a white paper. Bella continued to look blankly at her. The young nurse's composure began to crack. In a strained tone, the nurse read the list of names, slowly, loudly. It was only at the end of the list that Ellen pointed to the top of the list and uttered a meaningless word.

"Sure, ok, I'll be right back." The nurse returned holding a small plastic cup and a second cup filled with lemonade. Bella tossed back the meds, swallowed the liquid, and opened her mouth. The nurse happily peered into Bella's open mouth.

"Thank you," the nurse uttered, clearly exasperated.

Out of the corner of her eye, Kate watched straight faced as Ellen walked directly to the trash container slightly out of the red faced nurse's sight and let the pills drop one by one into the plastic liner. Bella blew Kate a silent kiss disappearing back to where from she had somewhere, somehow emerged, all the while humming through a self-assured grin.

PART OF THE CREW

Today was the day: day four for Kate. It didn't mean much but Kate was going to breakfast with the residents. The wind whipped wildly over the over the barren plains this morning. Wrapped up and buttoned down, the scraggly group formed two lines and walked slowly, heads bent against the wind. The men folks in the crowd dutifully lit up or tried. Hank fell in by Kate's side while Brenda took up the rear. The privilege of the dining room had been kept from Kate but she was neither looking forward to the new experience nor willing to continue to be excluded from the exercise.

The dining hall was very simply a cafeteria. The occupants were maybe a little unusual but not exactly different. Warming stations were set up on each side of the room. Residents stood in line waiting patiently for their segmented trays to be filled. Choice was taken out of the equation not because it was a challenge for residents, but because funding and dietary requirements dictated what and how much was allocated for each resident. For some the provisions were more than they had seen outside the walls, but for a few it was less than what they needed to maintain an amped up metabolism brought on by use or abuse.

Eggs, toast, and a piece of fruit were on the morning's menu. Kate filed through the line beside Hank, and she was sure to smile and thank her servers. The elderly farm raised women that passed out the morning breakfast put her in the mind of elementary school cafeteria ladies. They smiled and put an allotted portion on the tray. If they liked you or judged a resident too thin, they might give a little smile while making a portion just a little bit extra.

Kate sat down at one of many tables in the large room. Hank and Brenda sat with her initially. A few minutes later, Redg, a new face to Kate, gravitated toward the table. There was not much discussion between them for the simple matter if they did have something to say, the noise in the dining hall kept the recipient from hearing. More importantly, none of them felt comfortable speaking more than general platitudes in front of others.

Midway through Kate's breakfast, the cafeteria ladies began taking up the steam trays in order to prepare for lunch. A murmur spread through the hall, "Left over toast for those who want it."

Kate watched a flurry of activity as residents rushed to mill around the ladies who tried to judiciously hand out the squares of brown white bread and stay out of the fray at the same time.

Kate beheld Ellen wearing a sunflower covered sweater in the cafeteria ladies' blind spot. She deftly and methodically filled the bulk of her top with the toast and jam cups on a tray waiting nearby. Feeling Kate's eyes upon her, Bella put her first finger to pursed lips momentarily then disappeared into the chaos. Breakfast was over.

On the return walk to the dorm, Kate decided she really did not want to spend the day inside. During breakfast the wind died down enough for it to be a nice, if not chilly, day. With Hank by her side on the return trek, back and she decided to take advantage of the situation.

"Hey Hank?" She ventured.

Hank swung his head around to look at her. "Yep?"

"Will you take a walk with me when we get back? I still need a partner."

"Yep, sure will."

The oddly matched pair cut loose from the ragged formation and headed to the sign out sheet waiting by door of the dormitory.

Late morning saw no wind on the plains. The Midwestern sun shone brightly in its climb to the top of an azure sky. Kate took the lead down the black asphalt road.

"Where we going?" Hank inquired.

"Oh, just over the hill to that patch of trees there." Kate pointed.

"What is it?"

"Just something I want to show you and I'd like to take a closer look at it myself."

"Hey, Kate, I want to ask ya a question if it's a'right?"

"Sure, go ahead, I can't say that I will answer it."

"Well, I just kinda wondered why you haven't hooked up with one of the guys here." Hank wondered out loud.

Kate made a snorting sound from stifling a laugh. "I've only been here three days and besides Hank, why would I hook up with one of the guys here. It's not like we could have a long lasting meaningful relationship. At best, I'd lose a lot of weight, cuz I'd have to give over all my meals. Besides, I'm engaged."

Jim pondered the answer. "So, what does he do?"

Kate took a little misstep, "He's a doctor." As soon as the words slipped out, Kate wished she could grab them out of the air.

Hank took the question further. "Oh, what kind of Doctor?"

"Gyno." Kate knew immediately this second was equally bad.

Without letting the idea hang long, Kate reversed the question: "How 'bout you Hank? Married?"

"Naw, I'm what you call a widower." Hank's voice became gruff.

Kate murmured her condolences.

"Lost Myra last spring. Sure do miss her sumthin terble." Hanks voice was very quiet.

The two crested the hill before the clump of trees.

Hank continued, "Sure has been hard since then."

The jumble of bricks and broken glass stood before them.

"What in the Sam hill is that mess?" Hank exclaimed.

"That is what Brown used to be, Hank."

"Sure glad it ain't no more." Hank mumbled.

The pair walked around the rubble, skirting stray pieces of mortar and wood.

Hank picked up an earlier thread, "So you say you grew up here 'bouts?"

"Yeah, but I left when I was pretty young."

"So what church you go to?"

Kate felt that she had escaped one trap to fall into a hole.

"Well, Hank, I don't really go to church anymore." She responded.

Hank grasped onto the rope and yanked hard. "Are you saved?"

Kate answered the question again without giving too much.

"If you are asking if I believe, yeah, sure."

Hank wanted more. "Do you pray?"

Kate slowly responded, "Well I used to, but not so much anymore."

Again, "Why not, iffen you believe. It's important to talk to God."

Kate felt caught. This was an ongoing discussion wherever she found herself. She was always hesitant to engage.

"Hank, you know I don't really believe God answers requests. He's not like Santa Claus. I don't think it's a blessing to ask God for more than we need when it leaves other with less."

Hank cocked his head to one side as to listen with a better ear while Kate continued, "I think he lets us work things out on our own. I mean he gave us all we need. We know what is right and wrong. Does he have to do everything for us too?"

"Hmm might be, Kate."

"Hank, don't you feel God like in your heart? Isn't he part of you? Or is he sitting on high watching and judging?" Kate continued.

Hank stopped mid-pace and stroked his stubbly chin. "I never quite thought about it that way. Kinda makes some sorta sense though. I'll have to think on it awhile."

The path had ended. The yellow dormitory waited for its wanderers. Kate and Hank parted ways at the sign in sheet.

Before Hank went into the secluded men's wing, he patted her briefly on the shoulder and said, "I felt safe walking out in the woods with you. I'll be praying for you, girl."

Kate smiled, "Thanks, Hank, I enjoyed it too."

FAMILY GATHERING

Nurse Smiley rapped on Kate's door. "Kate, get up come to the day room. Don't bother getting dressed."

Getting dressed wasn't a choice for Kate yet. It only meant that she would be able to wear her robe over her raggedy jeans and summer shirt in the common area. She did as told.

Kate found her way to the main room where the residents of the dorm were deposited around a well-lit, twinkly, sparkly tree. "Oh yeah, Christmas," She reminded herself. Somehow, Kate had lost track of time. She clearly remembered a dry turkey breast, which she enjoyed alone. She had dealt with a sheared lug nut which kept her from going home.

Faintly, she remembered passing her dinner disguised as sandwiches to worn out travelers resting under a nearby overpass close to her apartment. Other than that, she recalled searching, and a miserable cold. The car trip had come later, but she didn't remember much but complaining at her drivers and their bickering with each other.

Kate sat at the edge of the group while Nurse Smiley passed out gifts from underneath the tree. Kate felt like she had accepted last minute invitation to a well-meaning acquaintance's family celebration. So she sat and watched the other patients open gifts. Some exclaimed with delight while others grudgingly accepted the gift. Nurse Smiley grabbed a large gift and tiptoed through the lounging patients then presented the gaily wrapped package to an angelic looking young man. His cottony black hair stood out of sorts. The young man slowly unwrapped the package, folding, and smoothing the paper in a neat pile beside him.

With sculpted delicate hands, he lifted the top of the white box which blocked the prize. The banter between the inmates hushed. A smile appeared tentatively on his face as the contents of the package was unknown to all, but him. He held his prize up for the room to see. The denim was dark blue almost black and the brass hasps shone brightly. The young man waded through the puddle of people that surrounded him. He disappeared only for a moment to reappear in an overall glory. The young face lit up with a sparkle that was not even matched by the lights on the tree. He was joyous.

Kate was a little envious. She saw his youth and his simple joy. She recalled that she had once possessed overalls which she also wore with pride. She remembered the denim of her youth. First, they were deep blue and sturdy. She wore the overalls so often that they eventually faded to a worn light blue. She had worked her overalls every which way. She wore them proudly until holes appeared at the knees.

Eventually, Kate cut the legs off and wore them as shorts. Somewhere in her passage into adulthood they became misplaced, lost or just merely tossed aside. She thought about replacing them now and then, but reasoned that she was beyond overalls just as she was beyond many other things. Kate sat on the edge of group mulling over her place in the world or anywhere for that matter. In the end, she decided she would not begrudge this young man's happiness and would try to find her place in that experience.

There were few gifts left under the tree. The festive spirit somehow lifted the mild gloom that pervaded its inhabitants. She felt somewhat at ease in being included in the celebration. Her recent holidays had been spent alone or in other hospitals where infrequent family get-togethers were overseen by orderlies and gifts where shabbily rewrapped after being searched by staff.

"Kate? Oh, there you are!" Smiley Nurse's smile was even brighter if possible. "Can you all hand this over to Kate?"

The nurse directed the patients lounging in between herself and Kate to ferry the bright foil package to its destination. The package was placed in Kate's own hands by Brenda who grumbled about being bothered on Christmas. Kate was surprised by the sudden show of generosity. She had counted only four days in Brown, but yet was remembered by the staff. Kate didn't care what the shiny boxed contained, she had been included. Kate thanked the nurse and placed the gift carefully on the carpet beside her.

"Aren't you going to open it?" Nurse Smiley nudged her.

"Oh, sure," Kate unwrapped the package under the watchful eyes of the staff. Inside the box she found a nightgown. The long thermal gown was thermal was covered with tiny red hearts from sleeve to hem.

"I was sure you could use that, Kate." Nurse Smiley said quietly then returned to passing out the remaining gifts.

Kate watched attentively while Nurse Smiley passed out the remainder of the presents. Kate felt a light hand on her shoulder.

"Kate, can you help me please?" Nurse Betty inquired.

"Sure, what do you need?" Kate asked.

"Well I need you to help me put away the leftover treats from this morning." Betty replied.

Kate followed Betty to a table which stood at the center of the room. Remnants of a light brunch were scattered all over the table. Bella hovered over the leftovers decked out in Christmas glory. Kate admired Bella's Rudolph sweater and shining golden ribbon cascading down her back. She thought, "If only," and then quickly "I'd never get out."

Kate and Nurse Betty somehow managed to clean up most of the crumbs and half eaten pieces of coffee cake and cookies the staff brought in for the residents. Bella unceremoniously put forth a great effort to beat the nurse and her charge to whatever food remained. Kate always enjoyed Bella's nimble way of purloining anything she desired even if Kate was the adversary.

As soon as the food was gone Bella disappeared to where she went with Betty and Kate dumbfounded in her wake.

"Betty, don't you think you should put some gloves on?" Kate mildly suggested.

Betty looked at the table top sans table cloth. The fake wood held a few glistening puddles.

"Oh no. The cloth is fine. No worries." Betty assured Kate.

Kate knew she shouldn't ask, but she was compelled.

"So what's going on with her?" Kate was almost embarrassed for prying.

"Oh Bella's been here for some time. She is schizophrenic. I have no idea where she came from. She was brought in one day by the police. She doesn't talk about herself or any family. As a matter of fact she doesn't talk at all. We have put her on diets and it doesn't work. She gets food somewhere. We don't know where. She doesn't take her medications. We know that. When we get her ready to be transfer to another facility, something happens and she no longer meets the criteria for one reason or the other. She seems to like it here and so she stays. She has made us her home."

DELIVERY

"Kate, come down here I have something for you today." Betty called to Kate from the business end of the nurse's station.

Kate walked to the opposite end of the long partition where she came face to face with a large brown cardboard box.

"This came for you this morning," the nurse smiled.

Kate reached for the box.

"Now, I'll open the box and you have to unpack it in front of me, Kate." Betty informed Kate.

For only minute, just one minute, Kate had forgotten her place and circumstance. She dutifully let the nurse break the seal on her box with a box cutter while she patiently waited to unpack it. Kate pulled out the jeans, shirts, and thermal underwear. Under Betty's gentle instruction, Kate shook the clothing to ensure that controlled items had not hidden in the clothing. Kate removed each pack of cigarette from the carton which she lined up by twelve soda cans that Kate also removed from the box.

Kate's mother had taken it upon herself to send the pop. Kate felt warmed by her mother's gesture. At the bottom of the box, Kate found a sealed envelope. Kate presented it to the nurse who waved it off, leaving Kate to repack the box subject for closer inspection in her room.

Kate dragged the box by the flap through the corridor to her room. Unlike any other day, today Kate was noticed. The care package was too big to hide. Women she had only seen during Med Time, found a reason to visit the facilities or look out the hall window to study the weather. It was unavoidable, just as unpacking it in full view of the other women would be. Kate tried to position the brown beacon at an angle behind the open door of the closet so she might have a little privacy with her package.

Kate shed her threadbare jeans. Quickly, she stepped into pair of her new ones. Her mother had sent two plain heavy shirts. She chose to wear the navy first. She folded the new clothes and put them in her seemingly empty suitcase. Lastly, she took the envelope from underneath her bra. Kate stepped inside her closet to open it. Her Mother had written simply on notebook paper, "We hope you get better Sweetheart," plain and simple. Kate hoped she did too.

A twenty dollar bill drifted to the floor. Kate scooped it up in her empty hand. Inside her closet, Kate took a simple inventory of her possession. Kate started with her clothing which appeared to have been safe. Then Kate turned to the top shelf of her closet. She counted 1-2-3 and 1-2-3...

"Shit!" quietly exploded out of Kate's terse lips.

So she reasoned. Someone knows how to pick fucking locks around here. Immediately she thought," I may not be washing my hair long, thanks asshole."

Not long after the box was unpacked the vultures began to circle. Kate heard a muffled knock coming from her door sill. She vacated the closet and stood in front of the closed door. The bright white orthopedic sneakers scurried across the floor of her room stopping squarely in front of Kate.

"Hi, Brenda," Kate greeted her giftee.

Without hesitation or salutation, Glenda fell into a story of need.

"I had five dollars in my wallet in my jeans last night and now it's gone. I've looked all over my room for it, but it's just gone. That's all the money I have. I don't how they could have gotten it. I've been in my room all this time. I didn't really sleep, so I would know if someone had gotten into my room............" the whine ran on.

At first Kate acted concerned, but as the story began to circle and the teller's voice became even shriller, Kate became increasing impatient. Kate's back was to the closet and Brenda blocked every path between her and the door. Kate slowly reached into her pocket for the worn bill that her brother-in-law had given her at the last loony bin.

"Here, Brenda, let me replace the five that you lost, OK. But you need to hear this, that's all you are getting from me from here on."

Kate knew as soon as Brenda's eyes locked on the bill in her hand, that her needy dorm mate heard nothing. The woman plucked the five out of her hand, smiled, and then exited faster than she entered. Kate mentally noted to make sure there was always distance from then on.

Kate turned the locked knob of the closet to be sure that it was indeed locked. Camped as she was outside of her room, she should have had the opportunity to watch the comings and goings. She had always wondered during her "vacations" how it was that a resident was able to slip in and out unnoticed. And yes, she had missed a lot of things only to find them abandoned somewhere else during her departures. She even had the misfortune to be accused during one stay and the consequences were harsh. Permanent lock down was torturous.

Kate had wished many kinds of fates on the young woman she consented to share a room with only to be nailed with a theft charge because the little bitch wanted privacy for her and her boyfriend. For Christ's sakes, Kate had even brought them sodas while they reclined on her bed. Fucking skank! Kate imagined that this artist was very skilled and had to be ... considering the consequences.

Upon her return to the dayroom, Kate found a new, but not new resident waiting for her. Redge, her dining companion, a tall thin man sat comfortably on the vacant couch. He nodded and smiled at Kate. Kate sat opposite the familiar stranger.

"You're, Kate, right?" In spite of his stature, Kate thought his voice was a bit too smooth and seemingly off pitch.

Kate did nothing, but nod her head in agreement. "I'm Reginald. We sit together for meals. Everybody just calls me Redge." Again Kate waited. "I was wonderin if you could give me a dollar for the soda machine and a pack of smokes. I'm good for it you know. I know what's coming and going around here. I might be able to help you out sometime."

Kate stood her ground while she greased the proverbial wheel. She disappeared only to reappear on the couch beside him. "I will not buy anything for you or give you a pack of cigarettes. This soda is yours and here are two cigarettes." She stated matter-of-factly. Redge's face contorted as he calculated the loss of a quarter and lucrative cigarette sales which were worth more than he could tote up mentally. He gathered quickly that something was better than nothing so he continued. "Are you married, got a boyfriend or anything?'"

Kate again nodded.

Redge checked Kate out from across the couch.

"Me I'm single, but I had me a girl, a big girl. You know long blonde hair. When she gets her checks we fill the grocery cart way up. All the way up to where it was hard to get the cart home without spilling. Yeah, it was a nice life.

Her folks didn't like me though. Kept pesterin her and pesterin her til we got in a fight and she left. Me I was mad. I busted everything up and yellin. Neighbors called on me. Now, here I am."

Redge smiled at Kate. It was a huge smile. Kate found herself smiling back and staring fascinated at something she never seen before. Regde might not a great guy, of course he tried to be smooth. It hadn't worked on Kate until he smiled. His smile was practiced, not genuine, but his left front tooth was blue. Kate watched his mouth closely while he continued, "Yeah, I likes me a big girl. You ain't a big girl. That's ok with me. We can't always get what we wants, but I can get you prit near everything you need here. Buy, sell or trade. You just come to Redge, hear?"

Kate sat fascinated with the flash of color as he spoke. "Hey, Redge. You know you have a blue tooth."

"Naw, man, ain't got no blue tooth. Got some color, but it ain't blue." He reassured his potential client.

Kate knew inwardly Redge was done with his pitch. She began to feel queasy and dirty at the same time, but she sat passively listening to him, watching for the blue to reveal itself and forbidding her hands to scratch the itch that popped up mysteriously all over her torso. She settled herself in the chair to stare for a while at her flickering screen, all the while hoping her perspective dealer would disappear. "Hey," a familiar voice broke in. Her smoke buddy poked his red nose around the corner. "Hey, Kate. It's time."

Kate thanked Hank and God together.

Cold days turned into bitter long nights. For the residents of building twelve, time passed quickly, but yet stood still. Paths were worn into the snow on the compound only to be melted by an unwilling sun. Dinnertime in the dining hall found Kate, Hank, Brenda, and Redge common companions. Kate habitually refused breakfast to recover from her early morning visitation, but the remainder of the day Kate's group dined together. As usual the more turnover the dining hall had seen the more it remained the same.

Brenda began the meal by updating the group on the status of her trust. Kate had heard many a plan to get sprung from whatever institution she had found herself in. They always involved a horrible guardian who was keeping the patient locked away. Money was the common thread. Yet, many patients hung onto the hope that they would magically be sprung. This was Brenda's daily tale. She put into motion a friend or relative who would push her greedy uncle off his perch thereby releasing her and her inheritance. Kate didn't know if in fact her story was valid, but Brenda's wealth didn't buy her new shoes or put five dollars in her pocket. Kate also knew it was easier to give her "her moment" at the table even if Kate ignored the monologue.

"Hey, Hank.?" Hank refocused his attention from his oven fried steroid enlarged chicken leg to Kate.

"You see that guy over there by that little girl?" Kate motioned to a tall lean bronze man barely of age.

"He's the one I told you about. You know at the New Year's dance. Told me he was forty-five like I wouldn't know the difference."

"Uh yup, looks like he found someone that doesn't."

Kate and Hank watched momentarily as Kate's prospective suitor sat near a skeletally pale young woman who stared off into space while her true love ate off of her tray and his own.

"See, Hank that's why you don't pair off in this place."

"Uh yup, jus so you know that, girl!" Hank turned back to the drumstick.

Screech! A metal chair slid across the worn linoleum. Kate and her dining companions turned to check the noise. In the center of the room stood a dark haired young man so unsure of his clothing arrangement or rather how his parts fit into his garments that he manually arranged the fit. The group watched in stunned silence as he checked the space in the back of pants by putting his hands between his skin and the material. In doing so he appeared to dislodge the fitting in the crotch of his pants.

With one hand, then the other he placed these fleshy parts back into the required material. Kate's table burst with laughter, but only briefly. Kate, Hank, and Glenda's outburst ceased as soon as it began. The three returned silently to their federally funded state provided recommended daily allowed chicken dinner. Neither glancing at the other, but focused downward.

"He has stepped up to the mound," Redge announced. "Yes, there is space. We have the ball!"

"Redge, it's not fucking funny." Kate hissed venomously without looking up.

"Yup, what do you think this is a damn Sunday dinner at home?" Hanks face was as red as the hand that gripped his fork.

"It is funny." Hank insisted, "This is like a dinner show."

The dinner companions glared at him.

Redge loudly scooted his chair from the table. "Fuck ya'll, I'm gonna watch me a show. I'm getting a front row seat. Fuckin moral majority sonbitches."

Redge carried his tray closer to the floor show. The remaining three wordlessly returned their tasteless dinner.

The residents of building twelve left the dining hall together. Two lines filed in and two lines filed back.

"Hey, Kate," Thin man caught up to Kate and shared a couple of paces with her.

"You know, Arkel?" He motioned to the owner of the coveted overalls.

"Yeah?" Kate replied.

"I wondered if you could talk to him?" he asked.

"Sure, what about?" she inquired.

"Well says he hears voices. I was wondering if you could help him. Just talk to him."

Kate was taken aback a little. Sure she could talk to him, but what do you say to someone who hears voices? Christ, she thought. Kate quickened her pace enough to gain a little on the young figure at the head of the line. Instead of calling for him to slow down, Kate caught his step and grabbed Alex's arm ever so gently, slipping her own through the crook. Arkel turned his head to see Kate.

"Hey Arkel, what's going on?"

"Oh, nuthin'."

"I really like those overalls." Kate said voicing a little light envy.

"Yeah, I like 'em too. Never had nothing new before. Spent most of my years in foster care."

"Oh, I didn't know." Kate felt stupid for her envy.

"It's ok. We got mostly second-hand stuff. It wasn't so bad, at least till high school." Arkel recounted the tale that was as painful to tell as it was to live.

"You've been hearing voices?" Kate fished.

"Yeah. Couldn't finish high school cuz of it. When I turned 18, I got sent here. I wanna get my GED, but…" Arkel trailed off.

"Well, Arkel, I don't know what it is to hear voices? What do they say?" Kate tried to steer Alex toward her target.

"Mostly bad stuff. Like scary stuff…telling me to hurt myself" Alex bit his lower lip. He pulled back the sleeve of his coat revealing a mocha wrist lined with dark colored slashes.

Kate recognized the marks.

"Arkel I don't have voices in my head, but I have these weird thoughts. They tell me lots of things that don't make sense, but when they are bad, they come really fast, so fast that all I can do is listen to them and nothing else. When they go away I'm so tired all I want to do is lie around and sleep."

"Yeah, me too," Arkel agreed.

"You need to just stick in there. We're safe here. It kinda sucks, but we're safe." Kate leaned in and hugged him ever so slightly.

"I like your hair." Kate continued.

"You do? It's kinda nappy." The young man began touching the small fro.

"Have you ever knotted it? " Kate asked.

"Naw," Kate saw that Arkel was contemplating the do.

"I'll do it if you let me?" Kate offered.

"What do you know bout folks hair, anyway." Arkel responded chuckling to himself.

Kate laughed back, "Oh I know a few things...just a few."

Laughter filled the main room. The winter sun cascaded through the bare windows. Kate gently ran a fine comb through her new charge's short black hair. Kate instructed her him calmly. Alex rested his back against the tan couch between Kate's legs. The positions they had taken caused the Walrus to keep a close eye on the pair from the nearby desk.

"Now before I get started, I want you to know I am not an expert at this and if you don't like it you won't hurt my feelings if you take it out ok? It's been awhile."

"Oh come on now, I'm just happy you're doing it." From his floor seat Arkel reassured Kate. "Where'd you learn to do it anyway is what I want to know."

"Well, I had a friend. She was much older than I was. Our kids played together and our husbands worked together. Anyway, she taught me a lot of things. She didn't tease me for not knowing something. She just kinda shook her head, chuckled a bit and then explained things." Kate's voice became soft and wistful.

"So what happened to your friend?" Arkel said into the air minding to keep his head still.

Kate paused while sectioning out her fourth square of scalp. "Oh, she divorced her husband and moved back to Boston."

"Do you ever hear from her?" Arkel asked.

"I did a couple of times after she moved, but that was a long time ago. I guess we just sorta lost touch." Kate responded.

"So, Alex, what about you? What are your plans from here on?" Kate inquired.

"Well, I have some things I want to do and some things I have to do." Arkel threw back.

"And what are they?" Kate pushed.

"Well, I have to get my GED. I missed too much school from being sick and all. This is my first time with adults. I've what they call, aged out of foster care, so when I get out of here I go to a halfway house. When I get my GED, I want to go to a trade school so I can get a good job." Arkel laid out his plan.

"Wow Alex that sounds great." Kate sectioned the crown of his head.

"Why do folks do that? Get divorced and break up and stuff and leave their kids?" Arkel voiced hidden anger.

"I don't know. Different people do it for different reasons I guess. One thing I do know, Alex, and this goes for us both... from now on we get to choose who we include in our lives and how long they stay there." Kate solemnly reassured both herself and Arkel.

Arkel cocked his head to one side. Kate's right hand held the blue fine toothed comb and her left hand rested on the young man's shoulder. For a brief moment they sat together: adult and child.

"OK...OK... you two are finished with your little hair styling session." Walrus had grown tired of monitoring the residents who to his mind were dangerously close to violating dormitory regulations.

Ignoring the large attendant's protests, Kate picked up the unit hand mirror placing it deftly in Alex's empty hand. "Now, take a look and tell me what you think."

Under Walrus' death glare, Alex carefully inspected Kate's work. He didn't see perfection in the rows of squares and knots. He saw maybe a few not so squared squares. But he saw companionship, and caring. It looked good in his eyes.

CAREFUL OF YOUR WISH

Kate went to sleep feeling a little self-important. She was granted her med request. Betty had proudly presented the two round tablets to Kate through the little window. As Betty she placed the med cup in Kate's outstretched hand, she called Kate's attention to the change while schooling Kate her on its side-effects.

"Kate, This may dry out your mouth so be sure to drink water continually throughout the day. Once you leave, remember too, no excess heat or sweating and be sure that you avoid acetaminophen, and Ibuprofen. Please check the interaction of any drug you take while you are taking this medication. We have scheduled your lab in six weeks. From here on out, you must have your level checked every six months. It's very important. Any deviation from this routine could be fatal. Understand?'

Kate's joy dimmed. Yes, there were risks, life was not without them. Kate tossed the tabs back washing them down with the ever present tart yellow liquid.

Nurse Betty swung her head back through the window, "Kate, one more thing. Don't expect immediate results. The medication has to build in your system to be at a therapeutic level. Just go about your business and we'll see how things turn out, okay?" Betty gave Kate a wink and then went on to the next in line.

Kate settled into her position on the floor after the march to the dorm. She gradually moved from the country video channel to an early morning documentary series. The other women had schedules to follow, but Kate was still new and had not been plugged into the system yet. She didn't mind; exposure to many people still put her on edge. Kate had slowly lost the desire to isolate herself, but hadn't yet found patience to deal with behaviors that brought out an irrational, aggressive side that was normally nonexistent.

Kate was happy to stay safe and warm after trudging through the foot of snow that fell on the grounds the night before.

She stretched and rolled the bear under the crook of her neck. A commercial for revolutionary injectable insulin played on the screen.

Christine poked her head around the corner of the day room just as Kate reached up to reposition her bear.

"Hey, Kate?" Christine softly called.

Kate decided at Christmas that Smiley Nurse was more active in her well-being than she had originally given her credit. Since the morning of the thoughtful gift, Kate had made an effort to include Christine. Whether Christine realized it or not, Kate had let her get closer just a little bit more.

"Yeah, Christine, what do you need?" Kate took her eyes off the screen.

"We aren't going to have a schedule for you until next week, but if you would like to get out and about, I know someone who could use your help." Christine had received a call early from the greenhouse informing the dormitories that there was an opening this week. When Christine talked to the grounds man, Kate immediately came to her Christine's mind.

Kate rolled from her back to stand on her feet. "Sure, Chris, that would be cool. What will I be doing?"

"I don't know exactly. All I know is that the grounds keeper need some help in the greenhouse for a while. What do you think?"

"Sure, I'd love to help in the greenhouse." Kate had to admit to herself that she would welcome a break from the hours of watching others.

"Get your things and I'll meet you at the desk." Christine slipped away.

Kate picked her way from foot step to foot step. Christine had given her a map of the grounds with her path highlighted in fluorescent pink. The nurse had seen the frown on her face, but waited for Kate's questions.

"You know, Christine, I once got in my car and headed towards the mountains and ended up in Portland. I can't find my way out a paper bag even with GPS." Kate voiced her frustration calmly.

"Well, Kate, I highlighted the way, but honestly, all you have to do is follow the footsteps in the snow. Once you get past the asphalt, there will be a path past the old hospital to the greenhouse. It sits in a little orchard. If you get lost, just stop a staff member and they will help you out. You'll do fine. No worries?"

Christine gave Kate a reassuring look and then shooed the hesitant woman out the door.

Kate could feel her toes become colder as Brenda's old sneakers soaked up moisture from the snow. She took care to step in the footsteps on her way to the barren orchard and kept her head down in fear of losing the sight of the breadcrumbs. Eventually, the trail ended at a rock candy pink covered yard. Kate threw her head up to view her destination.

The wind escaped her lungs. Kate recalled seeing a building like this only in books. The greenhouse, she surmised, had been leftover from the days of the original hospital. The glass panes shone like crystal in the dim winter sun. The architecture was obviously Victorian, complete with beautiful iron scroll work joining the entry to the deep arches of the building. The building made Kate wish she could see the original hospital, just the architecture, not the day to day she reminded herself.

"Hi, are you Kate?"

A bearded man filling the age-old description of gardener greeted her amidst her shock and awe. Kate shook herself mentally and physically only then finding a voice to respond.

"Yes, I'm Kate. I'm here to help." She spoke tentatively.

"Hi, Kate. I'm Ben, the groundskeeper. My assistant is away for the holiday and I'm running a little behind so I'm very glad you are here. Let's go on in the greenhouse, okay?"

"Sure." She breathed.

Kate was even more impressed once she stepped across the threshold. The floor was covered with a deep layer of twinkling pink crushed gravel. She could not see the entirety of the open house because it was filled with rows of shelves bursting with plants and flowers.

Ben allowed the amazed woman time to visibly peruse the area. When she was ready, he called her over to a row of open tubs and wooden tables.

"Are you ready to get started?" Ben inquired.

"Sure, what do I need to do?" Kate asked while taking her coat off. The temperature of the green house was a lot warmer that the temperature outside. Kate started to sweat.

Ben motioned to Kate her to move to a nearby work table. On the table stood a large rectangular tray filled with sand and a pile of cuttings. Next to it laid a flat container with a white powdery substance.

"What I need you to do is," Ben picked up a cutting and dipped it in the white substance, "dip the cutting in the rooting hormone," he put his finger in the sandy tray and made an indention large enough for the cutting. "Then put it in the sand and secure the cutting. What do you think? You got it?"

"No problem." Kate had already established two cuttings in the tray before Ben had finished his instructions.

"Well, Kate, you seem to be doing fine. I've got some other things to take care of, but I'll be around if you need anything."

Ben walked away.

"If you finish before I get back to you, I have some more cuttings and rooting hormone for you," he said before disappearing behind a shelf.

Kate set to the task. She had done it before in her own home. That was when she had a household to run. Lately, she didn't even have a house plant. Halfway through the pile of cuttings, Kate stopped briefly to remove the first of two shirts. Humidity combined with physical activity was something that Kate had not experienced in quite some time.

She felt a little low as she placed the last red tinted succulent in the third tray. The work went quickly. Ben strolled by nonchalantly in the guise of not checking up on her. Kate didn't mind. She had found a rhythm in her work which helped her to process the events of the last several months.

Kate remembered that things had gone well for her, very well in her mind. She had found a nice apartment on the edge of the city. She had picked up a new contract that promised eight months of steady work. Her children had found a solid path to her door. And she was dating, not a great guy, but she was dating. Most of all she picked up on old friendships while and even established new ones. Then the holidays hit and found her unprepared to meet an empty schedule in an even emptier home. "Fuck the holidays," Kate swore vehemently under her breath while shoving the last slightly crushed slip into a sandy hole. Kate carefully covered the plant's white tip while positioning the seen end to stand in line with rest.

After completing her task, Kate wandered around the green house. She noted projects and plants which were meticulously cared for. She found Ben sitting at desk built in a coarse wooden desk. Kate guessed it had been built from worn-out shelves.

"Hey, Ben, I finished all the cuttings," she said Kate informed Ben when he acknowledged her presence.

"Good, if you want to come back tomorrow, I have more."

"You mean the trays that that were on the shelves?" Kate asked.

"Yeah."

"I did those too. Is that alright?" She was a little afraid she had overstepped.

"No, Kate, that's great. Now we can get some other projects done that I didn't think were possible. There's always plenty to do." Ben assured her.

"So, can I come back tomorrow?"

"Of course, I'll be looking for you."

Ben turned his attention to the stack of papers and Kate quietly let herself out.

After the third day of greenhouse duty, Kate found her way easily. She also picked up Ben's method of organizing of the working materials. Each day Kate worked longer hours, spending more and more time away from the cocoon of the dayroom. She had often heard one resident or another mention the possibility of a paid job. She never paid much attention to what other residents said. It was mostly rumors and speculation if not pure delusion, but she thought, as it was her last day in the green house, and she might be able to parlay it into a more permanent gig, if not a paying one.

Kate set to planting ornamental flower seeds for landscaping. She knew it was tedious work as she looked from row to row of pots, but it was something she had always enjoyed. True, she had never tackled anything quite so large, but working this past week had engaged her body and her mind. She wasn't stemming on anger or her loss. Kate was productive instead of hiding and waiting for something that would never come again.

"Hey Kate, I brought you a soda. Let's take a break for a bit, okay?"

Kate covered a seed and brushed the remaining dirt from her fingers. Ben sat down in his old wooden swivel chair and pushed a stool toward Kate. She picked up the soda from the orderly desk and sat.

"So, today is your last day." It was more of a statement than a question.

"I guess, I was hoping to get...kinda like a permanent position with you...if possible?" Kate knew she was obviously fishing.

"Well, Kate, my assistant is coming back tomorrow and we don't really have any funding for anyone with your status. The positions are held for, shall we say, more permanent residents. Even then we don't have any openings."

Kate tried to keep her disappointment from showing.

"Besides, from what I understand, you won't have much time to spare. You are on what's considered the fast track here. I know it doesn't seem like it, but you won't be around long enough to see the spring flowers bloom."

Kate knew Ben was clueing her in, but the loss of the short-lived stability of the greenhouse hit hard.

"Ben, can I ask you something?"

"What do you want to know?"

"We all know why I'm here, but why are you here?" Kate knew this was probably not the question to ask staff, but she was curious. Why would someone as knowledgeable as the master gardener want to be in Podunk, USA, managing a bunch of lunatics, except for the world class architecture?

Ben planted his feet firmly on the pink gravel floor. He faced Kate directly and began.

"Well, Kate, I moved here when I eight. My father and I were living in Topeka. We would drive here every weekend to visit my mother. She was Schizophrenic. My father took the job of Master Gardener here so we could live close and be part of my Mom's life, whether or not she knew we were here. We were still a family in his mind. Anyway, I worked with my Dad on the grounds until I was old enough to be employed by the hospital. My Mom passed away and when my Father retired, I tried to fill his shoes. I guess I feel this is where I belong."

Kate processed Ben's story and saw an opportunity for more questions.

"Ben, can I ask you a few more questions?"

Ben nodded his head without looking back at her.

"I mean, my family is having as rough a time as I am…especially, my kids. Did you blame your mother for her illness? I don't mean to pry. It just seems there's a lot of blame going around even me."

"No, it's fine, really. I was pretty young so I guess when I was little, I just didn't understand. But as I got older, I went through a lot. I was ashamed, and I didn't want the kids at school to know about my mom. So, I would make up stories about her. You know…kid stuff about how we'd bake cookies or that she would tell me stories at night. I s'pose it was a way to include her in my life. I know I had a lot of anger for a while especially when I was 11 or so. I was so afraid it would happen to me. But as I got older and saw my Mom struggling to get better only to relapse again and again I saw how difficult it was and how much she just was hurting too. I knew then that all I could do was love her for who she was and not what I wanted her to be."

"What happened to her?"

Kate wanted to suck the words back into her mouth as soon as they were out.

"I would like to tell you she passed in her sleep in her later years, but I can't. When I was around fifteen, we lived in town at the time and she would come home with me and Dad on weekends sometimes. One Christmas, she very depressed and I insisted she spend Christmas with us. I thought it would help, you know?"

Kate nodded an understanding.

"Well, I got up early. I was excited about opening presents and such. When I went into her room to wake her up the bed was empty. Dad and I searched the house, but couldn't we find her. So, I went to get my coat out of the front closet to search outside, and that's when I found her. She had hung herself in the coat closet."

Kate let out an audible gasp. "I am so very sorry I asked. I just had to push. I'm so sorry Ben to make you go through it again." Kate wrung her hands and stared at the crushed pink gravel floor.

"No, don't feel bad Kate. It happened. That's my story. You know we all have one and yes, I miss my mom, but I had her lot longer than everyone thought I would. I guess I'm here mostly because of her. I see her here. A lot's changed since then. But still, I think I help in my own way."

Kate tipped the can of soda back and wet her tongue with the dregs of her pop. Ben lined a row of potted baby succulents along the edge of his desk. Kate counted five.

"I am gifting you with the fruits of your labor." Ben announced. "I can't pay you for your hard work. You helped me do some catch up. I can give you these little guys from your first day to remind of your time in this old grand dame."

Kate walked back to the yellow brick dormitory carrying a bag full of green and hope.

THE GIFT

Kate sat on the women's day room sofa tapping Brenda's gray shoe while flipping through cable channels. The dorm was empty except for her and two staff. Daytime television no longer held her attention. Her friends had a routine and she was, again, left behind.

Nurse Betty sat beside the impatient Kate. She took Kate's free hand in hers. Kate turned to her, hoping for a task.

"Kate, do you remember when you first came here and I explained the rules to you?"

"Yes, why? Have I broken one?" Kate queried.

"No, you haven't. Do you remember me explaining to you about the residents in orange?" Betty responded.

"Not really." Kate replied.

"Well, the people in the orange jumpsuits are here on campus, but they are not a part of our program. They belong to a different one." Betty hesitated briefly. "Kate, I have a request to make of you. If it's alright," the nurse began. "There is a resident who would like to give you a gift. Now he's not part of our program, but he's asked if he could give you a gift. It's up to you whether you accept it or not."

Kate had many questions for Betty, but knew she would not answer them. Patient information was confidential most times. Kate gathered that this was one of those times.

"Sure, ok. It's ok."

Who was she to turn down a gift?

"He's waiting for you outside the entrance. I will walk with you to the door and wait inside. If you feel uncomfortable, you just come back through the doors and I will handle everything else. Are you ready?"

Kate followed the older woman through the building to the double glass door entrance. On the other side of the door, stood a baby faced balding man in an orange jumpsuit. Kate turned to Betty with a questioning look.

"It's ok, Kate. Betty reassured her. "I will be right here. All you need to do is talk to him for a minute. This is more for him than it is for you."

Kate passed through the glass barrier to greet the awaiting stranger. He studied his feet until Kate spoke.

"Hi, I'm Kate." Kate offered her hand as the man change his focus to her face. "I was told you wanted to meet me."

The man seemed reluctant until he grasped her tiny hand in a huge mitt. Just as suddenly, he dropped his hands as he looked over Kate's shoulder in mind of Kate's protector.

"Uh huh, my name's Kenny. I know you don't know me, but I seen you around and you remind me of somebody I used to know. And well, I work a lot round here. I've got more stuff than I need. Anyway, I ain't never going any place else so I figured I should help other people."

Kenny reached to the singular back pocket in his orange jump suit and pulled out a hand tooled leather wallet. He thumbed through the bills and deftly fished out a twenty. "I know you got things that you need, so I'd like to help you with that."

Kate had so rarely been given anything in her life without feeling indebted. Brown seemed the last place where she would learn the art of acceptance. Kenny gingerly placed the bill in her right palm. She brought her left hand over his orange clad shoulder.

"Kate, we're on a schedule."

Nurse Betty spoke calmly yet firmly through a crack in the doors.

Kate stopped mid hug and politely thanked her benefactor. Betty safely ushered her charge into the security of the dormitory.

LIBERTY

Kate hadn't noticed the bridge on her initial trip to Brown State Hospital, but she saw it up close on her way into town. The bridge was an architectural feat. The facility was encased by a deep river. It was the only structure that crossed the divide. Residents and nonresidents alike called it the Freedom Bridge. Beyond the bridge lay the small town of Liberty. Passersby wouldn't guess the meaning, but today Kate clearly understood.

To Kate's mind, Liberty appeared to be no different than any other small Kansas town. It did have one remarkable feature. Liberty housed the largest discount store in five counties. The building sat on the edge of the community pushing the small frame houses to the edge of unfettered fields. The massive structure separated the farming community from the townsfolk. Kate studied the corrugated green metal building warily.

The people of Liberty milled in and out of its automatic sliding doors as they straggled through the huge parking lot pushing carts of purchases or setting their eyes on the sights that were held within. The good folk seemed to know neighbors as they waved and greeted those coming and going. Kate couldn't remember when she'd seen such goings on, but as always became an observer rather than a participant. Surely, she thought the townspeople knew the truck, therefore they also knew more about her than she did of them. Warily, she followed Percy into the giant store. Today he led two similarly looking women to the shopping cart rack at the entrance.

"You have an hour to shop. I will be here at the entrance if you need anything. The rest is up to you ladies." With that the women were released to wander, look or buy. Without taking notice of the other, Kate and her counterpart went their separate ways.

Kate really didn't know what to do. She strolled leisurely looking at baby clothes. She checked out the teeny tiny diapers that reminded her of paper napkins.

"No more babies for me...," she stopped herself before the pain set in. Kate pictured the closet of her new bedroom. In the very back the small closet, on the left side of the shoe rack, stood a small unpainted dresser. The top drawer held Amanda's baby clothes, the second held Annette's and the third held the clothes of the one who never came.

Kate sighed audibly and pushed her cart to the grocery aisles. It put her in the mind of a past life. She had always enjoyed weekend grocery shopping, the planning, and providing for her family. And the constant reminder that now she had no one to buy for, no one to feed. At the end of the row, she picked up a box of chocolates calculating mentally that for marked down merchandise, they were really expensive. Kate reasoned this was fun money, and she would use it as such.

In the near distance Kate saw a red sale sign. She worked her way through the maze of shelves to find herself in the shoe department. With further inspection she found a prize.

Nurse Betty's clogs lay in the bargain bin. Kate's find had a price. Her twenty dollars would not cover the purchase of both the chocolates and the shoes. What to do? Her shopping partner approached Kate and her dilemma.

"Did you find anything yet?"

"Yeah, how bout you?" Kate probed.

"Oh, I'm just getting a few small things."

Kate scanned her partner's cart and found a small bag of peppermints, with a container of dental floss.

"Um, I have a bit of a problem. Maybe you can help me?" Kate calculated.

"What is it?" inquired her partner.

"Well, I really want to get these shoes, but I don't have enough. Since you know Kenny gave it to us, maybe you could loan me a couple dollars."

"Well, I'd like to, but I've got stuff going on at home. I really need every little bit I can get. Honestly, you wouldn't believe how much this is helping me out."

Kate suddenly felt embarrassed for asking. She could only imagine how greedy she looked. Yes, she had been given free money, but she also wanted someone else's.

"Crap," she thought, "I need shoes, what the fuck am I doing buying blowing money on candy?"

It was decided, the rich, dark, endorphin producing shit would go back on the shelf. She would spend her money on the coveted leather clogs. It wasn't a difficult decision.

Percy patiently waited for the women to purchase their items. Frequently, folks stopped to pass the time of day. After Kate's clogs were scanned and paid for, she found a place beside the small bespeckled man. From time to time Kate feigned interest in the parking whenever a townie or friend stopped to pass time with Percy. Kate wasn't being shy or coy, but simply didn't want to be seen as the latest psycho from the loony bin that had been let out for a stroll.

The return from Liberty seemed quicker than the trip there. Percy remained his quiet, but friendly self. He pointed out landmarks along the road. Kate strained her neck trying to catch every little sight, but saw only what appeared to be hills and fields studded with occasional farms. She grappled for understanding of her earlier embarrassing behavior. She turned to her mirror image and introduced herself.

"I don't think we know each other's names. I'm Kate by the way."

The other woman turned her head away from the rolling plains and replied

"I'm Jill. Nice to meet you. I'm pretty new here."

"Again, Jill, I'm sorry if I put you on the spot. I wasn't thinking."

"Oh no, don't worry. It's just that I've been out of work since fall and my son and his girlfriend are taking care of my house."

"So, what do you do, Jill?"

"I'm a nurse, or was. I've been working third shift for I guess the last 10, 15 years. So, I guess I'm a little burned out."

"Third shift? Yeah, that would do it." Kate agreed.

Percy listened to the conversation while he drove another extra block home. Their driver unlocked the door so that Jill and Kate could carry their purchases into the dorm without waiting for other staff to admit them. Together they walked through the rooms and down the women's hall. The women continued to chat. Jill stopped at the room next to Kate's.

"Hey, I didn't know that you were next door to me all this time."

"I guess we are closer than we thought. I'll see you later, Kate."

"See you."

Once inside her room, Kate kicked the overly worn clammy shoes into the corner. She carefully pulled her new acquisitions out of the white plastic bag. Kate slipped the comforting clogs onto her small feet, admiring the fit and newness of smell. Her comfort led to confidence. She headed toward the desk, which was being manned by Walrus.

"Excuse me?" Kate began, trying not to look him in the eye.

"Can I use the phone?"

"What do you need it for?" he inquired, looking for more information.

"I need to call family," Kate replied.

The staff member couldn't find any excuse to extract more information from Kate, so he relented. Kate dialed her home number and then stepped away from the desk for privacy. Walrus moved to the end of the desk closer to Kate.

Kate phoned her apartment weekly, but hadn't been able to contact her daughter. With every call she left a status report of her progress on the answering machine. In lieu of verbal confirmation, Kate also periodically checked her finances to ensure that her home had been maintained.

"Hello?"

Kate immediately recognized her youngest child's voice.

"Hey, Ann, what are you doing there, honey?"

"Oh, hi Mom. Well, Dad's house got a little too small." Ann reluctantly confessed.

"I'm so sorry, Honey." Concern stood tall in Kate's voice.

"No, I'm sorry, Mom. Manda and I talked about it. We're both sorry. We just didn't know what to do."

Kate could hear a heartfelt apology in her youngest daughter's voice.

"It's ok, Ann," Kate reassured her child.

"Oh, Mom before I forget, a lady from your work called. She wants you to call her." Ann purposely passed on the important information.

"Alright, just give me her number."

Kate's daughter gave her a number that she recognized from work which was followed by a long pause.

"Ann, I love you. We probably need to get off here. There are others waiting."

"K, Mom, love you, bye."

Walrus blatantly loitered around the green phone. Kate replaced the receiver and held the tears for her room.

RE-EDUCATION

Phase three found Kate looking at a weekly schedule. Even after Thin Man explained the time blocks and pointed out the map of the grounds. Kate thought that she had less information afterwards than before the follow through. The waiting crowd passed through the open doors and Kate solicited help from those who made eye contact. Their explanations left her even more confused. Hank, the name popped into her head. He would know. Another fifteen minutes passed before Kate burst into the class room.

"I'm so sorry," she gasped.

A youngish looking woman leading the class directed a cold glare at Kate. While Kate searched for an available chair she heard, "Excuse me, are you supposed to be here? Ma'am, Miss?"

Kate heard a noise in the background, but continued to hunt. She did not notice a burly looking orderly and the strange worked up woman were closing in on her.

"What? What did I do?" Kate knew the two rushed in, but she didn't realize the reason.

"Do you have a schedule? If you do will you please show me?" The orderly asked.

Kate withdrew a crumpled folded white paper from her back pocket.

"Can you please open it and show me where you are supposed to be presently?" the woman commanded.

Kate unfolded the paper with the print for the woman to see.

"And you are Kate?" she inquired.

"Yes."

"Please show me this room number, the day and time."

Kate pointed to the first square on Wednesday's block. This woman was Ms. Schaeffer. The class was titled "Medication Administration."

"Alright, Kate welcome to our class. You didn't miss anything. We were just discussing how important it is to take medication regularly."

"Thank you Mrs. Schaeffer." Kate continued to stand.

I'm sorry, but you see, we are short on chairs. I hope you don't mind standing for a short time."

Kate moved closer to the table to lean. During the class she learned what a medicine dispenser was and how to load said dispenser. Mrs. Schaeffer's coverage of setting an alarm clock was noisily interrupted by a low loud moan at a back table.

"It's too goddamn hot in here! Turn down goddamn heat!"

A khaki covered woman charged Mrs. Schaeffer who unwittingly dropped the brass manual alarm clock she held up in front of her audience.

From Kate's vantage point, she saw braids, coffee-colored breasts and desperate fingers ripping at the zipper of a drab grey heavily insulated flight crew jumpsuit. Totally unprepared, the attending orderly wrapped the woman's exposed body in whatever loose material appeared available on the suit. Somehow he managed to instantaneously subdue the woman. Silently both disappeared from sight. Mrs. Schaeffer picked up the dented clock off the floor,

"We must be sure to set our alarm daily."

Without missing a beat, the lesson continued.

Later that evening Kate sat on the end of the sturdy flowery day room couch. She watched the World News while resting her chin on the snuggled bear. She had found a new interest on the goings on of the outside world. Most evenings she sat alone while the other women milled in and out of the room. She glanced at wall clock and read ten minutes until last break.

"Kate, you ain't gonna believe this, girl!" Redge made sure is presence was known despite the booming program.

"Hey, Redge." Kate replied without moving her eyes from the screen.

"Hey, you said you liked Arkel's overalls, right?" Redge was winding up.

"Yeah, so?" Kate had one eye on the TV and half an ear on Redge.

"Look what I got. Here's your overall!" Redge spun his pitch.

"No, Redge. I'm not buying those." Kate argued sternly.

"I can make you a good deal."

"No." Kate said sharply.

"They are warm and not much worn. C'mon Kate only twenty bucks or make me a trade? You got that pretty gold ring there."

He pointed to her thumb.

"No way, they are not what I was talking about. No, Redge."

Kate turned her back on the sale, preferring to watch rain totals in the Pacific North West than to watch Redge fold up the drab green insulated flight crew jump suit. Then she thought, or hoped rather, that Redge would leave her alone so she could enjoy her program.

"Hey Redge, you need to wash those things before you try to sell them to anyone else."

She lectured Redge in an abrasive tone. Finally, she heard him exit her space and called after him, "At least let them air out for God's sake? Ya hear?"

Kate was sure her voice had fallen on deaf ears.

Kate waited for last call, but then heard a whirlwind coming towards the day room. A small group of staff moved slowly through the hall.

"Jill, just breathe. In and out, in and out. Look at me. Look straight ahead."

The scuffle snapped Kate's chin off of the cuddly soft bear. She spotted her newly acquired friend in the middle of the commotion. Kate stood to get a better understanding of the situation. Jill from what she could see was having difficulty breathing. The panic in Jill's eyes told Kate that she thought she was not getting enough air.

No matter how hard she tried either she took in too much air which increased her panic or her panic increased the intake. Jill was hyperventilating, but that wasn't the reason she couldn't breathe. Kate recognized the familiar struggle and pushed her way through the crowd to reassure her friend.

"Jill, it's alright. You're safe here. You're Ok." Kate reached to pat Jill's back, but the touch was blocked.

"Kate, we got it. We are taking care of Jill." The women from the on duty staff guided the frantic woman into her room. Kate felt impotent, recalling past anxiety attacks and the fight to breathe. She could not help her friend. She only hoped that she could help herself.

NEW DAY

Somehow this morning, Kate realized, she had skipped the dream. She awoke early in the chilly dawn and sat at the empty chrome table. The dorm was quiet. Kate couldn't turn on the TV until the rest of the women woke. She wondered as she sat alone, why she had missed the dream. Was it because she had woken up before it appeared or that she had possibly grown beyond it.

Hank sat outside the women's hall waiting for Kate to emerge from her room. The two had gotten in the habit of walking to the snack bar during any free time. Hank always insisted on buying Kate's hot chocolate, along with his enormous cup of coffee. They walked the grounds when the weather and time permitted.

He remained her smoking buddy. Hank would become concerned when she ran low on cigarettes and would try to give her some from his coffer. At first Kate accepted, but then, after discovering how potent Hank's smokes were, she paced her own supply even more carefully.

As Kate passed Jill's door, concern nagged at her. Kate knocked quietly, "Jill?"

Kate gently opened the door and peeked into a still darkness. There was no response.

"Hey, Jill, we're going for hot chocolate later. Do you want to come?"

"No, thanks." Jill whispered.

"I'll just get you some. It'll be cold, but I'll bring you back some."

Kate could do no more.

"I don't have any money for you, Kate." Jill pointed out more distance. "I'll, take care of it. Don't worry."

This was all the reassurance Kate had to offer.

"Hey, Kate, thanks." Jill had given up her protest.

"Rest well, Jill." Kate offered up a little condolence.

"Hey, Kate. C'mere."

Hank was doing his best to get her attention without breaking the rules. Kate met him in the entrance of the woman's hall. The two were approached by country music's greatest fan. The man stashed his half-filled spit can under a cushioned chair and left a yodeling goddess to talk. This was the first time Kate had seen the wiry man vacate the glow of the country music station. It was Kate's turn to wait. Kate strained to hear the conversation, and between the singer's twirling chords, she only made out the words: almost broke, bloodsucking, and the name Redge.

"What did he want?" Kate was curious about the lanky man. Other than female country singer worshipping, all she knew about him was that he had found a way to feed his tobacco dependency without going outside.

"Aw…. he just wanted me to get him a cheeseburger at the snack bar. Seems Redge has pretty much drained him dry." Hank informed her.

"How's that?" Kate asked.

"Well, seems he cashed his check before he came here, but he eats a lot. He's purty skinny."

"So? How's that a problem?" Kate was perplexed.

"Well, he don't have access or nothing, so ever time Redge gets him a sandwich or sumthin there's a charge." Hank tried to clear up her question.

"What kind of charge?" Kate probed further.

"Oh, could be a sandwich or a pop. After a while it adds up. And he's about busted."

Kate could see Hank's frustration.

"Well, tell him I'll do it for free." Kate pronounced.

"Naw, don't work like that Kate, can't" Hank shook his head.

"What's he gonna do?" Kate asked.

"Don't know, I'm just wondering how his wife and babies are doing." Kate read worry in Hank's furrowed brow.

"C'mere, I got something I want to show ya." Kate followed Hank, quietly into an adjoining room.

"You're not s'pose to be in here, but I'm leaving today. What can they do anyhow?"

On the table in the room lay several books, a legal tablet and a pen. Hank picked up a well-worn leather bound book.

"This is my bible. I read one passage a day. And I write down any questions I have about it, and I try to work 'em out. This here's a little journal. I want you to write your address in it. I write Myra a letter ever day, I figured in a while, I'd start writing you too. Now, not everday. Just sometimes."

Kate scratched her address in the little book.

"Anyway, when Myra was still here, she would make me breakfast ever morning real early. We'd eat breakfast together and over our second cup of coffee we'd talk. We'd talk about the day ahead. What the Lord held in store for us."

"Hank, that is so nice," Kate sighed.

"Well, yeah, I kinda missed that. I jus shut myself up in the house. Didn't see nobody or talk to nobody. I kinda forgot about my kids and my grandbabies. Ya see, I forgot that I still had family and they missed Mama too."

"I'm so sorry you went through that, Hank." Kate lightly touched his arm.

"So, you are leaving? What are you going to do?" She asked

"My sons have kept the family business going. Now that I'm better, I'm gonna go back to work. And I'm gonna move in with my son and his family," Hank concluded.

"Wow, that sounds great, Hank." Kate found a little envy in her heart and hoped it didn't show in her voice.

"Now, I have few things to give you, my dear."

Jim Hank started picking through cans and boxes that surrounded a battered microwave. "Here's a can of hot chocolate mix and a couple boxes of crackers. The coffee I'm gonna give to the guys. Sides, you don't drink coffee anyhow. Now, I know I used some of this stuff, but it's still good don't fret," Hank counseled his friend.

"Oh no, I'm sure it's fine. Thank you, Hank." Kate reassured her friend.

"Now, you be sure to take care gitting them things to your room. Don't you let that Redge see you." Hank cautioned.

"One more thing I wanna say, now you know I'm evangelical."

Kate responded to Hank's announcement by theatrically rolling her eyes. He chuckled lightly,

"Now girl, ya know you're the only one that can pull that nonsense without lighten me up."

Hank placed himself squarely in front of Kate. He took her hands in his.

"As much as I want to see you in California, you know, see the ocean and all that. I just don't know iffin I can make it. If I don't see you again in Cally, Myra and I will be waiting for you in heaven. Just know that."

To alleviate the difficult good-bye, Kate stood on tip toes and gently placed a soft kiss on her departing friend's cheek. Kate realized that morning she could find her room blindly.

VISITATION

Kate found herself studying the leaves on the branches sheltering what weeks earlier had been a maze of dirt paths surrounding a pit. Wild grasses hid most of the materials that once housed patients like herself. Many of these patients lived the entirety of their lives within the walls that now lay led before Kate. She wondered how her life would have been had she lived only 60 years earlier.

Kate knew patients still received shock therapy and many were glad of it. Some even looked forward to it. And yes, sometimes her thoughts had raced so fast that she would have done anything to turn it off. She could imagine how those who had gone before her, gave in, maybe welcomed the relief. This was not the answer, at least not for her. The dream was gone.

She almost didn't notice as entrenched as she had become in the lives of others. Kate knew that she would never see her friends again, but that was not important. What was important was that she go on. Kate had walked past the asphalt road. At her feet lay the old. She glanced over her shoulder to check that she was in sight of the ward. The ground was wet in many places. Here and there patches of new clover sprung up from the dormant earth. The trees surrounding the abandoned wreckage budded new leaves where caterpillars had begun to eat and spin.

Kate reveled in the promise of spring, renewal. She sat down carefully in the fresh smelling hill of green and removed her prized clogs. She stripped her feet of the binding cloth then sunk her unpainted toes into the cool, moist cushion. Kate heard a noise. She listened closely. Kate could make out singing, but could see no one. Her eyes traced the path and found a small figure at the end bending down and standing up.

Kate felt starved as she took in the precious movements of a small child performing the simple yet all-consuming task of making a bouquet. She stifled a giggle as the pale blonde child plucked a much sought after wildflower only to drop two. The performance went on and on until Kate felt she could take it no more.

As if sensing Kate's presence, the child looked up from her last pick. Kate tried her best to look friendly, and not scare the poor child off. She gave the child a small she hoped warm smile and waited for the child to approach. Slowly, Kate thought probably out of curiosity, the girl drew near.

"What's your name?"

Kate was warmed by the direct question.

"My name is Kate. What's yours?" She replied.

The girl looked at her pudgy pink toes. Her face was hidden by a drape of fine cotton colored hair. All at once Kate felt two gray eyes as big as saucers looking directly into her own.

"I'm not s'pose to tell." she charged.

Kate detected the hint of a lisp somewhere in the two glorious sentences that this nameless waif shared. The girl put aside her flowers and sat beside Kate on the green mound. They both curled their toes through the clover and looked up at the sky.

"Do you have kids?" little Miss No Name inquired.

"Yes, I have two girls."

"What are their names?"

"Amanda and Annette."

Little Miss No Name clutched her stomach while rocking back and forth giggling. Kate knew this giggle and Kate giggled with the little imp without knowing the joke.

Holding back her joy, the child forced herself to say, "A net that is a funny name for a girl!"

Surprise hit Kate like a weight. Soon both of them were giggling until the giggle turned into musical peals of laughter.

"Well, where are your girls?"

"Oh, they are very far away."

"Do you miss them very much?"

"Very much."

"Why don't you get them to come here."

"Oh they are very grown up now and don't need their mommy as much anymore."

The gray eyes studied Kate face.

"Do you know a song?"

"Yes, I do. There is one my mommy used to sing sometimes to me when I little. Would you like to hear it?"

"Yes, please."

Kate looked onto the recesses of wild growth. Without thinking she sang very quietly.

> I'm a lonely petunia in onion patch, an onion patch
> I'm a lonely little petunia in an onion patch and all I do is cry all day
> Boo hoo, boo hoo,
> I'm so lonesome that it takes my breath away
> Right away
> I'm a lonely little petunia in an onion patch.
> Oh won't you come and play with me? (Godfrey, 1948)

Kate could feel a heavy quiet emanating from her audience. Both child and adult studied their toes.

"Kate, was your Mommy sad when she sang that song to you?"

"Yes, I'm sure she was sad sometimes. Everyone gets sad sometimes."

"Kate, are you sad?"

"Well, I was sad until I saw you."

"Kate, don't be sad anymore, OK?"

"OK, I'll try really hard not to be sad."

"Don't you know a happy song?"

"Hmmm"

Kate dug deep into the memories of her children's childhood and then brought something from her own that she had shared with them on spring days. Her voice was light almost cheerful.

"Snail, snail, come out and be fed
First your feelers, then your head
Then your momma, then your poppa
We'll love you forever." (Variation)

Little Miss No Name jumped to her feet and wiggled her pink little piggies in the clover; she put one pudgy little hand on Kate's cheek. Smiling, she looked deeply into Kate's eyes and began to sing Kate's childhood chant. Kate returned the childish intimacy and reluctantly watched as the small figured skipped down the path into obscurity.

"We'll love you forever," echoed in Kate's ears and her heart as she walked the black asphalt trail to her solitary home.

The days rolled by, the wind warmed by the sun trailed through the maze of buildings. Kate sat across the hall from the med room. She swung her feet in and out of the brown clogs which skidded across the pads of her bare feet. Kate had met with the social worker several times in order to scrawl her name across the bottom of her information release forms. It seemed they wanted more and more information of her recent hospital stays. Kate surmised that collecting was all that had taken place.

Her days at Brown had drug and then somehow blended together. Every night she wondered if that particular night would be her last night in the painted cinder block room. Day ran into day. Nothing had changed, but winter into spring. Her job, probably by now, long gone and her connections with the outside to the point of being severed. And yet she sat on the chair in the hall and hoped.

The sound of rustling papers echoed down the hall. Ms. Tuft, the always exasperated and disheveled too busy woman, rushed into her office and shut the door soundly. Kate continued to sit. The afternoon was quiet in the dorm. A few of the men lounged in the open day area and the staff relaxed in chairs behind the counter. Weather no longer prevented the remaining residents from strolling on the grounds.

"Kate? Can you come in here for a minute please?"

Ms. Tuft looked extraordinarily busy today. Her plumpish eyes were even plumper to Kate's own. Kate sat down in the only empty chair available across from Ms. Tuft's mound of case files decorated with multicolored sticky notes. The woman plunged a plump little hand into the pile and waved a manila file dotted with pink in front of Kate.

"Now, this is your file Kate. It says that you are from California. According to our agreement with that state, we cannot release you to return to that state unless we have family members agree to your return. Do you understand this? "

Kate quickly remembered her manners for an occasion such as this,"Yes, Ma'am."

Ms. Taft continued, "If your family members agree then we will provide transportation to your home state. However, if any one of them do not, you will be released in the state of Kansas."

"How long will this take, this agreement?" Kate searched.

"Possibly two weeks. Not more than three." Ms. Taft responded.

"But then I will get out?" Kate suppressed her excitement.

"Yes, but first you need to sign these papers and they will be sent in the morning mail. I'll get back to you when we have more information."

Kate searched the woman's face, but could not see a promise there.

She followed the little pink arrow at the bottom and signed her worthless signature. Yes, she thought it is possible, but probable?

Kate took the opportunity to walk the grounds. Her footsteps were a little light, but not too much. She thought of those she depended on to return home. It wasn't very likely that they would not want her back. She had her apartment. She had been able to maintain that. How could her ex-husband deny her return? She wasn't living with him. But if they cared would she be here? Honestly, she thought if anybody cared, would Brown State Hospital have any patients at all?

Most of her fellow patients were at the end of the line. Many had run their insurance into the ground, leaving their families no way to support them, or their families had just run out of steam, exasperated by their loved ones inability to get better. And a few seemed to cling to the security that was offered here and nowhere else for them.

Kate came to the hill. She saw the old building once again. The ruins reminded her of the old stories she had heard. On a day like today she imagined a line of men and women supported by a wrought iron fence firmly entrenched in their white straight-jackets standing like lilies decorating the yard. Yeah, she imagined, it's not so far off. The visible jacket is off, but the medical one...just a minor alteration. Yet, Kate sat and stared at the rubble. This little patch of ground had drawn her. She often sat in the very same spot on warm afternoons since Hank left.

"Do you mind if I sit down beside you?" she heard a youngish woman's voice ask behind her.

Kate continued to gaze into the foreground, "No, go ahead. I don't mind."

"You know they say it's haunted, don't you?" said the voice.

Kate chuckled and said, "No, I'm haunted. Those people don't care anymore."

"Really? What are you haunted about?" the voice became a body sliding denim clad legs out beside Kate.

"Oh, lots of things...kids mostly." She offered.

"Why kids? Any in particular?" Hands appeared on the knees of the voice's jeans. They were nice hands, young hands.

"Girls with golden hair and lots of promise and a boy who promised more than he could give." Kate heard herself become wistful.

"Why should you worry about them? Aren't they kind of like ghosts?" The voice's arm reached around Kate's shoulder and hugged her ever so gently. The young woman's head leaned gently on her shoulder. Kate felt an affection that she had gone long without. A simple touch from a simple soul. The two women sat for a long while, then walked together back down the black path.

Kate had her slip. She had earned her piece of paper at last. Today and only today, she would walk from classroom to classroom. In each classroom she would ask the instructor to sign off on her reeducation classes or so she called them. In the past months she had learned to apply for disability, measure and refill medications, and weave baskets. Yes, basket weaving 101 as her father liked to call it. None of these would help her overcome the challenges ahead, but she was taught the basic tasks of the mentally ill, who were in many ways treated like the mentally challenged.

None of it would get her a job, nor would it help further her education. Yes, sir, Kate was right on track. She was not a castaway, but a throwaway. And she was proud. How do you put resident of Brown State Hospital on your resume and get a job, a decent one? How many jobs are available for the mentally ill? Could she be a Healthcare Professional? Security Officer? Kate wracked her brain. She had to stay in Kansas, but her apartment was in Cally.

Kate's bank account was running pretty low these days. She hadn't the nerve to check the damage lately. It was made quite clear that she wasn't welcome, by what once was her family. Kate fished out a cigarette and lit it. She walked and puffed and thought. Kate stopped at the Arts and Crafts building or rather Therapeutic Recreation Building. Kate laid the burning cigarette in the butt tray. She was too preoccupied to spend time outside the building finishing her nail, but Kate was in no way going to waste a cigarette.

Letta waited patiently at the counter in the empty craft hall. Kate could never understand why the building was always so empty and quiet. She liked the place though. It didn't take her time to blow through the scheduled crafts. Letta always seemed pleased with her work. The instructor continued to order more projects for Kate and encouraged Kate to work at her own pace.

The kindly woman seemed to Kate to be much like her grandmother. She was gentle and encouraging even if your basket leaned more to the left than it should. Yes, Kate would miss Letta. Kate was not very crafty, but knew the value of it. Kate's teacher signed the paper slowly and wished her good luck. Kate touched Letta's calloused hand and with a gentle squeeze. This was her last stop before packing. After closing the A&C door Kate walked up on a twisted tiny man standing near the butt tray smoking. Kate snuck a glance at the empty tray. She raised her hand in a greeting and walked on by. Poor guy, he must have needed it more than I did, she thought sadly.

"I hope you don't mind if I sit here for a little bit?" Nurse Betty's voice broke into Kate's thoughts.

"No, go ahead. I could use some company." Kate replied.

She often sought her spot on the clover covered hill. Kate found the sight restful. Staff and resident alike knew where to find her during free time. Kate enjoyed conversations while gazing at the vegetation that partially revealed the ruins below her spot. Often she enjoyed the peace and solitude alone.

Since Kate had arrived at Brown, she had thought of nothing more than leaving. Now that it was approaching, she felt unsettled about what the future held.

"That's good, real good, Kate." Betty touched her shoulder and momentarily paused.

"I think spring has sprung. Too bad Hank didn't see it. But it's better for him to be home." Kate found herself reflective mood this afternoon.

"How bout you Kate? Is it better for you to be home?" Betty questioned.

"Depends on which one. Neither one really wants me. They don't know how to deal with me." Kate knew her reality.

"How's that?" Betty lightly pushed.

"They can't reconcile the person I was…you know strong and capable to the one who was angry and irrational. My family has moved on without me and I'm still trying to figure out how to fit back in the world." Kate put bluntly.

"Yeah, but what happened? You woke up one day and decided this was the day to escape reality?" Nurse Betty urged Kate on.

"No." Kate was suddenly guarded.

"Was it the baby?"

"Fuck, she is going there." Kate thought, "Maybe?"

"Tell me Kate, tell me what happened. You're the only one who knows."

Betty had a small detail of the closed woman's history. She pushed at the crack in Kate's composure.

Fuck, fuck, fuck! Kate screamed inside her head. She knew her medical history would finally catch her out. Nurse Betty was the one to ask the question.

Kate felt obligated to her for the kindness she had shown. Yet, she felt put upon because the nurse dug into an unspoken hurt buried deep within her.

"O. K. Since you won't let it go. Here it is." Kate spoke angrily. Her voice mechanically spat the facts.

"I got pregnant about four years ago. I was really happy you know? My children were leaving home and I would have another baby. I wouldn't be left alone. Their Dad wasn't especially happy about it." Kate saw herself moving about the house with a disengaged voice nagging, harping at her while she performed daily chores.

"Then the debates started at dinner then…at bedtime. I couldn't escape. He kept pestering and pestering me. We were too old, we already had our children. It was too risky, something might be wrong with it. I didn't care. I wanted my baby more than life itself. I needed it. I would have given my life for it. Even if something was wrong with it, I wouldn't have loved it any less. Anyway, I finally got fed up with the nagging… I caved. Even though I refused to get rid of the baby, I did agree to testing…to have an amniocentesis. I figure it would get him off my back if nothing else."

Kate paused to check herself and then calmly continued.

"I'll never forget it. He was away on business like he always was. The kids were doing what they did. So I went by myself. The procedure was quicker than I thought it would be. I was pretty scared, but the Doctor told me it went well."

Kate's voice cracked in the middle of the sentence. She gulped down air to finish her story.

"Anyway, on the way home I started bleeding… just a little. So, I drove myself to the E.R."

Kate barely felt Nurse Betty's hand on her shoulder or heard the nurse murmur words of compassion.

"By the time I got to the ER, I had already miscarried. Spontaneous abortion….that's what the medical report said. That's what they called it. They said the needle nicked the placenta and I lost a perfect little girl. Why? Doesn't matter. I lost my baby all by myself."

Kate sat as still as stone. She steeled herself for further questioning.

"What about your husband?" Betty was riding her hard.

"Oh, he was really concerned at first. At least he tried to be. I couldn't be out of his sight without him continually calling. I couldn't get away…like find even a little bit of peace…like solitude to just be still and think. Then one day we had a horrible argument. I couldn't stand be continually watched and having him hovering over me all the time. We had a horrible argument over not just the baby, but years and years of stuff. I stormed out to my car just drove. I just drove and drove. I guess I got stopped or something cuz I ended up in the hospital. That was my first break, it was hard for him… them."

Kate hesitated briefly.

"It went from not being able to be anywhere on my own to where I could be gone for weeks at a time with no one noticing until I landed in the hospital again."

"How 'bout now, Kate?" Betty was in for the finish.

"Now? Oh, he has a new baby now. Nice for him, huh? I didn't even know he had a fucking wife." Kate tried, but could not keep her animosity in check.

"What about your kids?" As much as Kate had avoided this moment she was glad was out..

"Oh, they're ok. Kids are resilient, you know?"

This was the one truth that bothered Kate so badly. Yes, her kids would do well. They would have a little more baggage than most, but she had taught them to be independent, even though at times she wished she hadn't.

The nurse knew how difficult this revelation had been for her younger charge. She also knew that the woman needed time to let go of the pain that she had carried so long with her. Betty gave Kate room to process the feelings that until now only churned ceaselessly in the recesses her mind, but one question nagged at her. Nurse Betty had her answer and wanted to know Kate's.

"Kate, can I ask you a question?"

"Yeah, sure, what?"

Kate's gray pain filled eyes met Betty's soft blue eyes. Kate's body stiffened in anticipation.

"Did you name your baby?" Betty gently inquired.

Kate's head snapped back then dipped forward showing the older woman nothing but the crown of Kate's hair. Betty noticed strands of gray amidst the coppery brown locks. She heard nothing, but saw the bowed figure before her slowly rise as Kate struggled to breathe deeply. The wall was crumbling. Quietly, Kate finally wept for her loss.

The women sat for a time on the hill. The landscaping was wild and green. The old and the new peacefully coexisted. A breeze picked up pushing Kate's shoulder length hair up into her tear stained face. She unclasped her hands reaching up to draw the plastered hair away. Kate gazed up into dusky sky and sighed from somewhere within her soul. She leveled her eyes so that Nurse Betty could see them, but did not focus on Betty, but on something intangible to them both.

Softly she whispered," Faith, Betty, I named her Faith."

MOVING ON AGAIN

Kate packed her bag. It didn't take long. Her thermals lay in the very bottom of the bag with her extra pair of jeans. The jeans weren't clean, but they weren't really dirty. Kate refused to guard the washer for 45 minutes and then hover over the dryer for another half an hour.

She was really surprised that she was leaving with both pair. She wore one of her two warm weather shirt. Kate remembered how she had to fight for a simple t-shirt that disappeared within minutes of arriving at the dorm. It was the only time she sought Walrus' help. She scanned the closet for additional articles left behind, out of habit. God only knew she didn't have much.

"God dammit to hell!" Kate yelled in the closed closet.

She planned to take a quick shower before bed. The scan revealed that she had not missed anything, but her last bottle of shampoo and conditioner were gone. She had spotted the third set a month earlier, but reasoned it unimportant knowing she had a fourth set waiting. Had this been her last day and she was walking out the doors, she couldn't have cared less. It wasn't. She planned to walk out of this hole better than she had stumbled in. Kate wanted to throw herself on the bed and just give up, but whatever she wanted to do tonight that choice remained unavailable. She could not, would not, do anything to close those doors. Kate did not know if she could be retained, but she did know that her exit was set in stone, sooner rather than later.

Kate found Nurse Betty standing at the desk. She smiled more warmly than Kate remembered. Kate stood quietly waiting for the elder lady to address her.

"Yes, Kate what can I do for you?" Her voice was warm.

"Betty, it seems that I don't have any shampoo and I would like to take a shower tonight," Kate was brief.

She offered no explanation and one was not requested.

"Come with me over to the surplus closet. When people leave, sometimes, they donate what they don't want to take with them. We should have some shampoo and maybe some conditioner."

Nurse Betty walked the length of the counter stopping at a door that in all the time that Kate had been in the dormitory, she missed. Kate followed the nurse into the unfamiliar closet.

"This is it. Do you see anything that you need?"

The shelves held toothbrushes and paste. She saw brushes, combs, half boxes of tampons, and an odd assortment of disposable razors. Kay's eyes locked on four bottles of shampoo standing with their corresponding conditioner. The bottles showed varying levels use. They stood in order of their disappearance.

"Go ahead, take what you want." Nurse Betty offered generously. Kate picked the first set that disappeared shortly after her arrival. Of course this was the best one, but not the most expensive. She pondered the loss for a moment and wondered. Was this the work of one person who traded or sold her goods for profit? Or had four individual residents crept into her room one at a time, picked the lock on her closet stealthily removing the desired object. Had the thief sold or used the hair products, the consumers donating them upon their departure.

Suddenly, Kate stopped stemming. How many people would go to such lengths to steal shampoo? When is conditioner as valuable as gold? At that very moment Kate put the criminal analysis behind her. She was beyond asking the where's and what fors of survival in Brown State Hospital. She was not a lifer, and no longer a willing frequent flyer. Kate promised herself that she would never again live where the windows didn't open and a locked door was an invitation to enter.

Nurse Betty allowed Kate to skip breakfast the last morning of her internment. Kate visited her haunt by the old hospital one last time. She could barely see the outline of the structure from her little mound. Masses of blackberries and wild vines covered the jutting walls. Dandelions had grown tall casting cotton parachutes every which way. The noises of late spring filled the air.

Kate listened closely as she tried to catalogue the sounds. She listened as prairie birds chirped and the humming of honey bees mixed with the sounds of untold others.

Kate did not hear the sounds of the little one. No happy giggling, no joyous laughter. There was no cotton top to follow or hope that there would be. Her

Faith was lost and in admitting that the one thing she most hoped for was beyond her touch.

Perched on the clover covered mound, Kate hugged her knees gazing forward. Out of habit she looked over her shoulder checking for the nurses' window. Reassuring herself of compliance, Kate's attention turned back to the past before her.

Kate pondered her experiences over the last four years. Yes, she had lost deeply, but she need not carry that loss. And yes, she did mourn her baby, her children and her marriage. Time for mourning was now over as was hiding. She carried her children with her every single day. They were as much a part of her as she was of them wherever they may be.

Kate leaned forward and plucked a huge sunshine colored flower from a massive cluster at her feet. She rubbed the cushiony petals at the base of her nose. Kate saw Faith's pudgy pink hands filled with flowers and heard the lilting giggle that had so often warmed her heart.

Kate sat for the last time in the small corridor between the doctor and social worker's office. Ms. Tuft asked her to wait there while she finished up Kate's paperwork. There was no clock visible to Kate. She was suspended in Limbo. Kate was no longer a resident, but also was not free to walk out the door. She needed papers to cross the line between the inside world and the much desired outside world. Kate could not leave alone. Regulation required an escort. So she sat.

"Kate? Can you please come in now?"

Mrs. Tuft put on her most official face and held a file before her. The file was strictly manila. Kate guessed it was her official file.

"Your ride just left the gatehouse. So we need to get started. Now, Kate, I have some papers ready for your signature. I need you to sign here. This is your discharge paper."

Kate tried to read the small black print, as usual, the matronly woman huffed and puffed to remind Kate that she had a very large caseload and very little time to spend on the individual case. Kate pushed the pen across the black line which was followed by many other papers with black lines. Ms. Tuft stapled papers and relined the folder with them.

At this point, Ms. Tuft only puffed. On the cluttered desk an orange plastic baggie proclaimed danger with the appropriate skull and crossbones. She handed it off to Kate.

"This is your medication, be sure to take it regularly. It helps if you take it every day at the same time, just a tip. Finally, be sure to contact a doctor or clinic to arrange follow up care. Kate, I think I just heard your escort. Can you please peek around the corner and ask him to come in?"

Kate stuck her head into the hallway. She found her brother waiting uncomfortably. The man shifted his feet from side to side, while he craning his head to monitor for moving objects. His eyes wide open proclaiming discomfort in the wake of curiosity. Kate motioned her hand towards the office. The poor guy stopped his jerking in order to move his feet forward and not fall flat.

Shep appeared in the door looking, if possible, even more uncomfortable in the confines of the small office. Ms. Taft waved the wide eyed man closer.

"Now, I need you to sign this form for me. Kate's steps were high and light. It states that you are escorting your sister off the grounds of the hospital."

Kate's brother bent over the paper and left his signature.

"Alright, Kate, we are finished. Please do not forget your copies and medication."

Kate tucked the baggy screaming danger into her waiting travel bag. She smiled to herself knowing her cuddly bear would be snuggled by a most beautiful caretaker. Her brother, Shep, carried the small black travel bag as any gentleman should. They departed the building not through the main doors, but through a rarely seen staff door.

She did not leave as she had arrived. Her hands were free. Kate's steps were high and light. Kate's departure went unnoticed by the new and the more settled residents of building 12. Shep's truck stood on the black drive shining red in the promising spring weather. He tossed the bag in the bed and climbed in the cab alongside Kate.

The long separated siblings fell back into a familiar pattern.

"So. What was going on back there, Shep?"

Her younger brother shifted gears into reverse and then first.

"Huh? Where?" He threw back.

"Back in the in the lobby. You looked like you thought they might make you stay," Kate teased.

"Hey, I wasn't taking no chances," he grinned widely.

Kate was happy to see the buildings change. The dark black asphalt road led them past the hidden rubble. Black turned to gray. Beyond the gates of the compound, fields displayed new growth hill after hill. Kate soaked in the vastness. Shep turned to his sister briefly.

"So, whatcha gonna do now?"

Kate shrugged, "Go back to California."

"But I thought you couldn't go back?" he asked.

"Well, the state said they wouldn't pay the fare unless my family agreed. That doesn't mean I can't go on my own."

Kate laughed at thought of CHIP's officers manning check points on the California state line.

"Where you going to live then?" Shep continued to ask the questions.

"There are plenty of places for me to live. There're lots of overpasses, bridges, and of course the beach."

The nose of the truck veered sharply to the right. Kate's little brother jerked the steering wheel in the opposite direction overcorrecting his surprise.

"What the fuck, Kate?" Shep's eyes blazed momentarily into hers.

Kate's laughter filled the cab. "Well it's not like I haven't learned anything, ya' know."

Shep's posture stiffened.

"No, it's ok. My signature is on the lease. My checks have been paying the rent. My car is there. I have an apartment filled with my furniture, with my clothes, my dishes, and everything else."

"But your family doesn't want you there. They said that in those papers."

"You know what, Shep? Only one person doesn't want me there. As far as I'm concerned my opinion is the only one that counts from here on. I'm better. My kids are ok. That's all that really matters to me. And for the rest...they will just have to deal with it."

Kate watched closely while the yellow brick of building twelve grew small. A mass of trees and clinging green vines blocked the old hospital from Kate's view, but she knew it was eternally there for her as were the many souls who had once again found a path. Kate knew how easy was to slip or lose her way, but she felt different this time......stronger...if possible...maybe even more sure of herself.

Brown State Hospital disappeared bit by bit in the red truck's side mirror and Freedom lay before her.

Kate's steps were high and light.